The Political Socialization of Black Americans

A Critical Evaluation
of Research on Efficacy
and Trust

Paul R. Abramson

THE FREE PRESS
A Division of Macmillan Publishing Co., Inc.
NEW YORK

Collier Macmillan Publishers
LONDON

The Free Press
A Division of Macmillan Publishing Co., Inc.
866 Third Avenue, New York, N.Y. 10022

Collier Macmillan Canada, Ltd.

Library of Congress Catalog Card Number: 76–25343

Printed in the United States of America

printing number
1 2 3 4 5 6 7 8 9 10

Library of Congress Cataloging in Publication Data

Abramson, Paul R
    The political socialization of Black Americans.

    Bibliography: p.
    Includes indexes.
    1. Afro-American children. 2. Political socializa-
tion. 3. Afro-Americans--Psychology. I. Title.
E185.86.A27   301.5'92   76-25343
ISBN 0-02-900170-6

*For my father
and in memory of my mother*

Contents

List of Tables

Preface and Acknowledgments

This study began as a paper presented at a conference on "Theory and Research in Social Education," held at Michigan State University in February 1971. The conference was supported by the United States Office of Education, which provided support for my paper under grant OEG-0-7-2028(725). The first paper discussed only four basic studies in racial differences in feelings of political efficacy and trust, but a second version reported differences in ten separate studies. Both these papers advanced four basic explanations for racial differences in feelings of political efficacy and trust. A shortened version of the second paper appeared as "Political Efficacy and Political Trust among Black Schoolchildren: Two Explanations," *Journal of Politics,* 34 (November 1972), pp. 1243–1275.

Since that article was published, numerous additional studies have appeared reporting racial differences in connection with these attitudes. Considerable new research on feelings of self-confidence has been reported, and this research forces me to modify my earlier social-deprivation explanation. In addition, since my article appeared several studies have explicitly tested my explanations. The present report discusses many additional socialization studies, presents all four explanations, and revises my initial social-deprivation explanation. Despite these changes, some of the material in this book is similar to previously published portions of my *Journal of Politics* article, and I am grateful to the Southern Political Science Association for permitting me to use this material.

Numerous scholars read and commented on earlier portions of this book. Among them are Charles F. Andrain, David V. J. Bell, Wilbur B. Brookover, Cleo H. Cherryholmes, Jack Dennis, Brian T. Downes, David Easton, Frederick W. Frey, Fred I. Greenstein, Timothy M. Hennessey, Robert D. Hess, Herbert Hirsch, Robert W. Jackman, M. Kent Jennings, John H. Patrick, Jewel L. Prestage, Harrell R. Rodgers, Jr., David W. Rohde, David O. Sears, and Paul M. Sniderman. I am especially grateful to Ada W. Finifter and Frank A. Pinner, who commented on an earlier draft of the entire manuscript.

This book would have been impossible without the numerous scholars who provided me with additional information about their research and, in some cases, allowed me to report research findings they had not yet presented. Harold M. Barger, Edward G. Carmines, Lee H. Ehman, Samuel C. Funderburk, Anne M. Heinz, William E. Hulbary, Dean Jaros, M. Kent Jennings, Kenneth L. Kolson, Merton S. Krause, Samuel Long, Jack K. Masson, Richard G. Niemi, Anthony M. Orum, Harrell R. Rodgers, Jr., Alden J. Stevens, and George H. Strauss provided me with additional information about their research. M. Kent Jennings also provided early information about the University of Michigan Survey Research Center's 1973 survey of high school seniors, and Lorn S. Foster provided me with early information about his research. Bruce A. Campbell, Marjorie Randon Hershey, and Samuel Long sent me unreported information about racial differences in studies they had conducted. Three scholars conducted data analyses on my behalf. Richard G. Niemi provided additional information about the University of Michigan Survey Research Center's 1965 study of high school seniors and their parents, Jerald G. Bachman sent reports about his panel study of tenth-grade boys, and Richard C. Remy provided information about his study of high school seniors.

I am also grateful for support from the Department of Political Science and the Computer Institute for Social Science Research, Michigan State University, and from the Institute of International Studies, University of California at Berkeley.

My wife Janet helped edit the manuscript and provided continual encouragement.

None of the above named individuals or institutions is responsible for my conclusions.

About the Author

Paul R. Abramson (Ph.D., University of California at Berkeley), Associate Professor of Political Science at Michigan State University, has written extensively on preadult political attitudes and adult voting behavior in Western Europe and the United States, and his articles on these subjects appear in numerous journals. Dr. Abramson's study of English schoolchildren was one of the first political socialization studies conducted in Britain. His earlier book, *Generational Change in American Politics,* contains analyses of black voting behavior, party identification, and political attitudes. His article and papers on black political socialization have been widely cited and have influenced subsequent work by researchers. This book is an extensive expansion and revision of his earlier writings on black schoolchildren.

PART I

Findings

INTRODUCTION

The seven million black schoolchildren in the United States, like their forty-two million white counterparts, have virtually no political power. Yet socialization research suggests that black children feel less politically powerful than white children do. Like white children, black children have little experience with which to evaluate the trustworthiness of political leaders, but research suggests that black children are less likely to trust political leaders than white children are. Feelings of political powerlessness and political distrust appear to develop among blacks even before they become adults. Why do such feelings develop?

To build theories about the differential political socialization of subcultural groups, we need to go beyond mere findings and progress toward developing explanations. Better research designs for future studies of socialization demand attempts to explain currently available findings. My goal will be to evaluate four basic explanations for the low feelings of political effectiveness and political trust found among black schoolchildren. Through this evaluation I will assess the theoretical and research implications of available socialization research about black Americans. Before we can begin our theoretical task, however, we must define our concepts, examine available research findings in some detail, assess the representativeness of these findings, and judge the reliability and validity of the measures used to study political attitudes among preadults.

Chapter 1. Feelings of Political Effectiveness and Political Trust among Black Schoolchildren

BASIC FINDINGS

Socialization researchers have studied a wide range of political attitudes among American schoolchildren.[1] For our purposes, however, we will concentrate on attitudes that have been studied by many researchers and about which theoretically interesting explanations can be advanced. Some interesting attitudes, such as compliance to authority, will not be discussed because too few studies have been conducted to establish a solid empirical base upon which to build explanations.[2] Other attitudes, such as the tendency of black children to identify as Democrats, are not discussed because, although such findings may be widely documented, they are not theoretically interesting. Two attitudes, feelings of political effectiveness and feelings of political trust, have been studied by many researchers. The frequent use of these variables partly reflects a tendency for socialization researchers to replicate measures used by prior studies, but these attitudes are, as we will see, central to socialization research for sound theoretical reasons. Moreover, as I hope to demonstrate, interesting theoretical explanations can be advanced to account for racial differences in feelings of political effectiveness and trust. Basic findings about feelings of political efficacy and trust can be summarized as follows:

Finding 1. Black schoolchildren tend to have lower feelings of political effectiveness than white children do.

Finding 2. Black schoolchildren tend to have lower feelings of trust toward political leaders than white children do.

DEFINITION OF BASIC CONCEPTS

By *black* I mean socially considered to be black; by *white* socially considered to be white. I employ Pierre van den Berghe's definition of "race." "We consistently use the term race . . . to refer to a group that is *socially* defined but on the basis of *physical* criteria."[3] Whether or not there actually are races in any biological sense is irrelevant for our purposes.[4]

Political effectiveness can be conceived as a norm, as a disposition to be effective, or as a form of behavior.[5] One views efficacy as a norm when one says that people should be able to influence political leaders. Efficacy is conceived of as a disposition when one says that people feel they can influence political leaders. And one views efficacy as a form of behavior when he discovers that people actually do influence political elites. Because the findings I interpret are about respondents who were too young to exert much real influence upon political leaders, I will examine only the first two meanings of this concept.

Since 1954 numerous researchers have studied feelings of political effectiveness,[6] but Robert E. Lane has presented one of the most imaginative treatments of this concept.[7] Lane interpreted political effectiveness as a conviction that the polity is democratic and that government officials are responsive to the people. Lane's conception has two components: the image of oneself as effective and the image that the government is responsive. In recent years political scientists have begun to emphasize the potential multidimensional meaning of the concept, and the measurement problems this poses—but this recent criticism has not yet affected most socialization research.[8] It seems safe to say, however, that collectively the items used in the studies I discuss tap both the dimensions specified by Lane. For the purposes of the explanations to be developed, I take the view that the items do not tap merely "regime norms" as to how political leaders should respond, but actual beliefs about effectiveness and responsiveness.[9]

Feelings of political effectiveness, of course, are not the same as actual effectiveness, yet they are important for two basic reasons. First, persons who feel politically effective are more likely to participate in politics and thus may be more likely to influence political leaders. Second, feelings of effectiveness seem to be related to other values that contribute to democratic politics. Gabriel A. Almond and Sidney Verba, for example, found that persons who felt they could influence political decisions were more likely to believe that election campaigns were needed and were more likely to believe that ordinary people should participate in politics. Almond and Verba viewed feelings of political competence as a "key political attitude."[10] Some might argue that it is more important to study actual participation, rather than an attitudinal propensity to participate. But children have virtually no opportunity to participate in politics, and the study of feelings of political effectiveness among children may serve as an indirect measure of their future propensity to participate. That black children have low feelings of political competence does not necessarily mean they will grow up to be nonparticipants; this will depend upon future events far beyond the scope of political socialization research. Moreover, that blacks score low on feelings of political efficacy does not mean that they are "undemocratic," or that they are somehow bad citizens. Indeed, unrealistic expectations about one's ability to participate may be as self-defeating as feelings of political despair. On the other hand, feelings of political effectiveness may be a political resource, for groups that feel politically competent are usually more likely to exert political influence. To some extent, the causal arrow between feelings of political effectiveness and actual political effectiveness may run in both directions. If so, low feelings of political efficacy among blacks may be partly a cause of, as well as a consequence of, the actual political powerlessness of black Americans.

Feelings of *political trust* have also been studied extensively, although there is perhaps less agreement about the dimensions of this concept.[11] Feeling that leaders can be trusted involves the belief that they will usually be honest and will usually act in the interest of the people. Feelings of trust may involve a belief that political leaders are competent. Some of the studies reported below directly asked whether political leaders could be trusted. Ten of the studies measured "political cynicism," which may generally be considered a reverse measure of political trust.[12]

Political trust and political efficacy are usually correlated. Persons who feel politically efficacious are more likely to trust political leaders than are persons who feel inefficacious, and the relationship between efficacy and trust among adults has been growing in recent years.[13] Some scholars view both feelings of political efficacy and trust as dimensions of a broader concept, political alienation.[14] Yet they are separate dimensions, as William A. Gamson makes clear:

> The efficacy dimension of political alienation refers to people's perception of their ability to influence; the trust dimension refers to their perception of the necessity for influence. Feelings of low efficacy and feelings that the government is not being run in one's interest are, of course, likely to be found together. If one feels he cannot contribute significant inputs he is likely also to feel unhappy with the outputs but this is an empirical hypothesis which might prove false under some conditions (e.g. pater-

nalism, nobless oblige). In any event, these two aspects of political alienation can be conceptually distinguished and the trust dimension refers to
beliefs about the *outputs* of the political system.[15]

Feelings of political trust may be more central to the study of political socialization than are feelings of political effectiveness. Feelings of
trust measure, at least indirectly, "support" for the political system,
and according to some socialization researchers, support for the polity
must develop fairly early in the lives of its members so that the system
will have a reservoir of "diffuse" support to draw upon if incumbent
authorities fail to provide satisfactory outputs.[16] According to David
Easton, support may be focused on one or more of three general objects:
persons may support the political community, that is, the broad group
of persons who share a political division of labor; the "regime," that is
to say, the basic rules of the game through which political power is
shared; and, last, the authorities, that is, the elected officials and
bureaucrats responsible for making and implementing political decisions.

Political trust has declined markedly during the past decade,
among schoolchildren as well as among adults. But this decline has far
greater implications if it reflects a withdrawal of support for the community and the regime, and is not merely a rejection of political incumbents. Arthur H. Miller, who has clearly documented the decline in
political trust among the American electorate since 1964 (as measured
by items quite similar to those used to study schoolchildren), argues
that "a situation of widespread, basic discontent and political alienation exists in the U.S. today."[17] "Such feelings of powerlessness and
normlessness," Miller maintains, "are very likely to be accompanied by
hostility toward political and social leaders, the institutions of government, and the regime as a whole."[18] The low level of trust among
Americans today, Miller suggests, may contribute to extra-legal political behavior, party realignment, and radical political change.[19] In his
critique of Miller's thesis, however, Jack Citrin argues that the recent
decline in trust probably reflects a withdrawal of support from the
political authorities. "The meaning of recent increases in the level of
political cynicism," Citrin concludes, "remains ambiguous, and to deci-
sively conclude that there exists widespread support for radical political change or pervasive alienation from the political *system* is prema-
ture, if not misleading."[20] Miller remained unpersuaded by Citrin's
critique, and specifically argued that the low trust among blacks reflects declining support for American political institutions, such as
elections, as well as a rejection of political incumbents.[21]

The questions raised by the Miller-Citrin controversy cannot be
resolved by examining the face validity of the items used to study

political trust among schoolchildren. But for the most part the items used to study schoolchildren (which are reported in full in Appendix C) do seem to focus on specific political authorities, rather than on either the regime or the political community. Still, it would be unwarranted to conclude that the low political trust among black schoolchildren merely reflects a rejection of incumbents for, as David O. Sears points out, Easton's analytical distinction between the community, the regime, and the authorities is difficult to measure empirically.[22]

It seems reasonable to hypothesize that the low political trust among black schoolchildren would be more likely to persist into adulthood if it reflected nonsupport for the community and the regime. But, even if we knew that black political cynicism had this wider meaning, we would have no reason to conclude that black children who are now politically cynical will grow up to reject the American political system. Like the future consequences of low feelings of political efficacy, the future meaning of black distrust depends on events that go far beyond the scope of political socialization research.

I must emphasize that political distrust among blacks is not necessarily bad, and I would not argue that blacks ought to trust political leaders. Blind trust in political leaders is scarcely healthy in a democracy. A skeptical, questioning citizenry may be necessary to check elite abuse. But the low trust among black schoolchildren may lead to future nonsupport among blacks as they become adults. Such nonsupport could lead to nonparticipation in conventional politics, further weakening the ability of blacks to influence political leaders, and to violent protest that threatens basic democratic institutions.

ELABORATION OF BASIC FINDINGS

Although few social scientists have focused primarily on the political attitudes of black schoolchildren, at least 38 separate studies,[23] yielding 45 data points, report on racial differences in feelings of political effectiveness, political trust, or both. They are summarized in Appendix A, in which the data are presented chronologically. The map in Appendix B shows the research sites where these studies were conducted, while Appendix C reports the questions used to measure these feelings, and the procedures used to build additive measures. Part 1 of the Bibliography provides the citations for the sources used to construct these appendixes, but in many cases the data are based upon personal communications, and I often present information not provided in the research reports.

Of the 30 surveys that report upon feelings of political effectiveness, 20 clearly found blacks to feel less efficacious than whites, while five others found blacks to be less efficacious on some measures, but equally efficacious on others.[24] Henry I. Penfield's study of Alabama schoolchildren found blacks were more likely than whites to agree that "voting is the only way that people like my mother and father can have any say about how the government runs things," but found no racial differences on three other questions commonly used to measure feelings of political effectiveness. Similar findings were discovered by the University of Michigan Survey Research Center's 1973 nationwide study of high school seniors. Jack Dennis' survey of Milwaukee schools found that blacks were as likely as whites to say they felt free to complain to local government officials, but they were less likely to feel that these officials would respond favorably to their complaints. And Merton S. Krause found that Chicago area blacks were less likely than whites to feel efficacious toward the mayor and toward the police, but found no significant racial differences in attitudes toward the president.[25] Last, Richard C. Remy's survey of high school seniors found blacks to be less efficacious than whites on most efficacy items, but found negligible racial differences on others.

One survey, conducted by George H. Strauss, also fails to fit the overall pattern. Strauss found that among New York City high school students there were virtually no racial differences in feelings of political effectiveness, but his finding is based upon a single item that he viewed as a measure of "understandability."

Only four surveys found blacks to be marginally more efficacious than whites, and three of them were based on atypical samples. James T. Jones' survey was conducted in Gary, Indiana, and his finding is based on a single question about the city government. Harrell R. Rodgers' finding is based upon a survey in Edgecombe County, North Carolina, which is poor and rural, and in which whites had far lower feelings of political efficacy than whites in the general population.[26] And Samuel Long's St. Louis study is based only upon students in inner-city schools. While Lee H. Ehman's study may be based on a more typical setting—a high school in Pontiac, Michigan—he surveyed only 41 blacks and 62 whites in his panel analysis.[27]

On balance, there is considerable evidence that black children feel less politically efficacious than white children do. Moreover, these racial differences in feelings of political efficacy do not seem to result from differential social background characteristics alone. In all studies in which blacks felt less politically efficacious than whites, and where controls for social background characteristics were introduced, racial differences persisted.[28] Despite some anomalous evidence, we do not need to modify Finding 1.

Findings about political trust are less consistent than those about political effectiveness. Blacks proved to be as trusting or more trusting than whites in four of the first six studies. Penfield's study showed blacks to be more cynical about Alabama political leaders than white children were, but blacks were much less cynical about federal government officials. Although Ehman's panel study found blacks to be less trusting of national-level officials, these differences were based upon a small sample. But blacks were less trusting than whites in 24 of 33 surveys conducted during and after the summer of 1967. Four other surveys provided some evidence that blacks were less trusting. Edward S. Greenberg's study of Philadelphia schoolchildren showed that blacks were less likely than whites to believe that the government in Washington could be trusted, although they were slightly more likely than whites to say the government never makes mistakes. Krause's Chicago-area study found that blacks were less trusting toward the mayor and the police, but that there were no significant racial differences in trust toward the president. Rodgers' Edgecombe County study found blacks to score somewhat higher on trust than whites, although blacks were markedly less likely to trust the police. And Long's study of Evansville, Indiana, high school students found blacks to score as slightly less trusting on Olsen's political discontentment scale, but slightly more trusting on Agger's political cynicism measure.

Of the five post-1967 surveys that failed to find blacks less trusting than whites, three were based on atypical samples. Once again, we find Long's sample of inner-city schools. Samuel C. Funderburk's study was conducted in Key Largo, Florida, and the Dean Jaros and Kenneth L. Kolson survey was conducted in a rural community near Middlefield, Ohio.[29] On the other hand, Jerald G. Bachman's survey was based upon a national sample of high schools. While there is nothing inherently atypical about Thomas J. Williams' Georgia survey, it should be remembered that his measures focused on national level authorities when Lyndon Johnson was still president.

Like racial differences on feelings of political effectiveness, differences in trust do not appear to result from differential social background characteristics alone. In those studies that found blacks to be less trusting, and in which social background controls were applied, racial differences persisted.[30]

It also seems highly unlikely that differences between surveys conducted before the summer of 1967 and those conducted during and after that summer result from accidental differences in sample composition. For the time-series trend suggested by separate studies of different samples is also supported by Bachman's panel study of tenth-grade boys, and by the two national surveys of high school seniors conducted under the direction of M. Kent Jennings. In the fall of 1966, Bachman found blacks to be more politically trusting than whites.[31] By the spring of 1968 political trust had declined among both blacks and whites, but political trust had eroded faster among blacks than among whites and racial differences were erased. A year later trust had again declined among both races, once again falling faster among blacks than among whites: blacks now scored lower on political trust than whites did. By the summer of 1970, trust had again declined among both racial groups, although slightly more among whites than among blacks: blacks still scored lower on trust than whites.[32] The national surveys conducted by Jennings and his colleagues yield similar results.[33] In the spring of 1965 racial differences were slight and inconsistent on the five questions used to measure feelings of political trust. (Racial differences were also negligible on a political cynicism scale used for a smaller interview-based study.) All five trust items were repeated in a large questionnaire-based study conducted in April 1973, and for both races political trust had dropped markedly on all five questions. But for every question the decline in trust had been greater among blacks than among whites. In the 1973 survey blacks were less trusting than whites on all five items, and on two items, including one that specifically asked whether the government in Washington can be trusted to do what is right, racial differences were marked.

The evidence from separate surveys of different samples, Bachman's panel survey of a national sample, and two national samples conducted by Jennings and his colleagues all suggest that a reversal in racial differences emerged during and after the summer of 1967.[34] Because of this time-series trend, we must modify Finding 2. Black schoolchildren have tended to have lower feelings of trust in political leaders in surveys conducted during and after the summer of 1967. Of course, that summer, which emerges as a turning point from our examination of survey data, is also historically significant, for it was the season when black riots were devastating major American cities.

NOTES

1. For recent summaries of this research literature, see Dean Jaros, *Socialization to Politics* (New York: Praeger, 1973); Richard G. Niemi, "Political Socialization," in *Handbook of Political Psychology,* ed. Jeanne N. Knutson (San Francisco: Jossey-Bass, 1973), pp. 117–138; Michael P. Riccards, *The Making of the American Citizenry: An Introduction to Political Socialization* (New York: Chandler, 1973); Robert Weissberg, *Political Learning, Political Choice, and Democratic Citizenship* (Englewood Cliffs, N.J.: Prentice-Hall, 1974); David O. Sears, "Political Socialization," in *Handbook of Political Science, Volume 2: Micropolitical Theory,* eds. Fred I. Greenstein and Nelson W.

Polsby (Reading, Mass.: Addison-Wesley, 1975), pp. 93–153; and Sears, *Political Attitudes Through the Life Cycle* (San Francisco: Freeman, forthcoming).

2. However, for two interesting studies that report racial differences in feelings of compliance toward political authorities, see Richard L. Engstrom, "Race and Compliance: Differential Political Socialization," *Polity*, 3 (Fall 1970), pp. 100–111; and Harrell R. Rodgers, Jr., and Edward B. Lewis, "Political Support and Compliance Attitudes: A Study of Adolescents," *American Politics Quarterly*, 2 (January 1974), pp. 61–77.

3. Pierre van den Berghe, *Race and Racism: A Comparative Perspective* (New York: Wiley, 1967), p. 9.

4. For a discussion of the controversy concerning the biological existence of races, see Leonard Lieberman, "The Debate Over Race: A Study in the Sociology of Knowledge," *Phylon*, 29 (Summer 1968), pp. 127–141.

5. For this formulation of alternative meanings of political effectiveness, see David Easton and Jack Dennis, "The Child's Acquisition of Regime Norms: Political Efficacy," *American Political Science Review*, 61 (March 1967), pp. 25–38.

6. Measures of "sense of political efficacy" were first introduced in 1954 by the University of Michigan Survey Research Center (see Angus Campbell, Gerald Gurin, and Warren E. Miller, *The Voter Decides* [Evanston, Ill.: Row, Peterson, 1954], pp. 187–194). The authors used responses to five questions to measure the respondent's "feelings that individual political action does have, or can have, an impact upon the political process, i.e., that it is worth while to perform one's civic duties." Numerous empirical studies have used essentially the same concept, although it has been labeled "sense of effectiveness" (see Elizabeth Douvan and Alan M. Walker, "The Sense of Effectiveness in Public Affairs," *Psychological Monographs: General and Applied*, 70 [Whole No. 429], 1956), "political potency" (see Robert E. Agger, Marshall N. Goldstein, and Stanley A. Pearl, "Political Cynicism: Measurement and Meaning," *Journal of Politics*, 23 [August 1961], pp. 477–506), "subjective political competence" (see Gabriel A. Almond and Sidney Verba, *The Civic Culture: Political Attitudes and Democracy in Five Nations* [Princeton, N.J.: Princeton University Press, 1963], pp. 230–236), and "subjective civic competence" (see Donald R. Matthews and James W. Prothro, *Negroes and the New Southern Politics* [New York: Harcourt, Brace World, 1966], pp. 275–280). Several authors have analyzed feelings of political ineffectiveness, and have used terms such as "political futility feelings" (see Arthur Kornhauser, Harold L. Sheppard, and Albert J. Mayer, *When Labor Votes: A Study of Auto Workers* [New York: University Books, 1956], pp. 155–165), "political anomie" (see Charles D. Farris, "Selected Attitudes on Foreign Affairs as Correlates of Authoritarianism and Political Anomie," *Journal of Politics*, 22 [February 1960], pp. 50–67), and "political incapability" (see Marvin E. Olsen, "Two Categories of Political Alienation," *Social Forces*, 47 [March 1969], pp. 288–299).

For two major attempts to refine this concept, see Ada W. Finifter, "Dimensions of Political Alienation," *American Political Science Review*, 64 (June 1970), pp. 389–410, and Edward N. Muller, "Cross-National Dimensions of Political Competence," *American Political Science Review*, 64 (September

1970), pp. 782–809. For recent methodological critiques, see Stanley Allen Renshon, *Psychological Needs and Political Behavior: A Theory of Personality and Political Efficacy* (New York: Free Press, 1974), pp. 31–41; George I. Balch, "Multiple Indicators in Survey Research: The Concept 'Sense of Political Efficacy,'" *Political Methodology,* 1 (Spring 1974), pp. 1–43; Herbert B. Asher, "The Reliability of the Political Efficacy Items," *Political Methodology,* 1 (Spring 1974), pp. 45–72; James S. House and William M. Mason, "Political Alienation in America, 1952–1968," *American Sociological Review,* 40 (April 1975), pp. 123–147; James D. Wright, *The Dissent of the Governed: Alienation and Democracy in America* (New York: Academic Press, 1976), pp. 89–110; and J. Miller McPherson, Susan Welch, and Cal Clark, "The Stability and Reliability of Political Efficacy: Using Path Analysis to Test Alternative Models," *American Political Science Review,* forthcoming.

See John B. Robinson, Jerrold G. Rusk, and Kendra B. Head, *Measures of Political Attitudes* (Ann Arbor, Mich.: Institute for Social Research, 1968), pp. 441–481, for a compilation of some of these measures, as well as for measures of political cynicism.

7. See Robert E. Lane, *Political Life: Why and How People Get Involved in Politics* (Glencoe, Ill.: Free Press, 1959), pp. 147–155.

8. See, in particular, Balch, "Multiple Indicators in Survey Research."

9. Given David Easton's analytical framework, a belief that citizens can affect the government is a regime norm (see Easton and Dennis, "The Child's Acquisition of Regime Norms"). But the items used to measure feelings of political efficacy among schoolchildren do tap beliefs about the responsiveness of political leaders and also involve an indirect assessment by the child of his family's ability to influence those leaders.

10. Almond and Verba, *The Civic Culture,* p. 257. Subjective political competence is the main dependent variable in Almond and Verba's five-nation study.

11. Among those studies that have examined feelings of trust among adults are: Robert E. Agger, Marshall N. Goldstein, and Stanley A. Pearl, "Political Cynicism"; Donald E. Stokes, "Popular Evaluations of Government: An Empirical Assessment," in *Ethics and Bigness: Scientific, Academic, Religious, Political, and Military,* eds. Harlan Cleveland and Harold D. Lasswell (New York: Harper, 1962), pp. 61–72; Edgar Litt, "Political Cynicism and Political Futility, *Journal of Politics,* 25 (May 1963), pp. 312–323; Herbert McClosky and John H. Schaar, "Psychological Dimensions of Anomy," *American Sociological Review,* 30 (February 1965), pp. 14–40; William A. Gamson, *Power and Discontent* (Homewood, Ill.: Dorsey, 1968); Ada W. Finifter, "Dimensions of Political Alienation"; Edward N. Muller, "The Representation of Citizens by Political Authorities: Consequences for Regime Support," *American Political Science Review,* 64 (December 1970), pp. 1149–1166; Jeffrey M. Paige, "Political Orientation and Riot Participation," *American Sociological Review,* 36 (October 1971), pp. 810–820; Edward N. Muller, "A Test of a Partial Theory of Potential for Political Violence," *American Political Science Review,* 66 (September 1972), pp. 928–959; Joel D. Aberbach and Jack L. Walker, *Race in the City: Political Trust and Public Policy in the New Urban System* (Boston:

Little, Brown, 1973); Richard L. Cole, "Toward a Model of Political Trust: A Causal Analysis," *American Journal of Political Science,* 17 (November 1973), pp. 809–817; David C. Schwartz, *Political Alienation and Political Behavior* (Chicago: Aldine, 1973); Arthur H. Miller, "Political Issues and Trust in Government, 1964–1970," *American Political Science Review,* 68 (September 1974), pp. 951–972; Jack Citrin, Herbert McClosky, J. Merrill Shanks, and Paul M. Sniderman, "Personal and Political Sources of Political Alienation," *British Journal of Political Science,* 5 (January 1975), pp. 1–31; James D. Wright, *The Dissent of the Governed;* Jack Citrin, *Political Disaffection in America* (Englewood Cliffs, N.J.: Prentice-Hall, forthcoming); and Edward N. Muller and Thomas O. Jukam, "On the Meaning of Political Support," *American Political Science Review,* forthcoming.

In addition to the studies summarized in Appendix A, feelings of political trust among preadults have been studied by Frank A. Pinner, "Parental Overprotection and Political Distrust," *Annals of the American Academy of Political and Social Science,* 361 (September 1965), pp. 58–70; Dean Jaros, Herbert Hirsch, and Frederic J. Fleron, Jr., "The Malevolent Leader: Political Socialization in an American Sub-culture," *American Political Science Review,* 62 (June 1968), pp. 564–575; David Easton and Jack Dennis, *Children in the Political System: Origins of Political Legitimacy* (New York: McGraw-Hill, 1969); and Paul R. Abramson and Ronald Inglehart, "The Development of Systemic Support in Four Western Democracies," *Comparative Political Studies,* 2 (January 1970), pp. 419–442.

12. Throughout my discussion, persons who score low on political cynicism are considered to score high on political trust. This seems a plausible interpretation, for the same items used to measure political trust are also used to measure political cynicism, sometimes by the same authors. For example, Kenneth P. Langton and M. Kent Jennings used a six-item political cynicism scale (see "Political Socialization and the High School Civics Curriculum in the United States," *American Political Science Review,* 62 [September 1968], pp. 852–867). But Jennings, along with Richard G. Niemi, used five of the same items, with the same data set, to construct a political trust scale. (See *The Political Character of Adolescence: The Influence of Families and Schools* [Princeton, N.J.: Princeton University Press, 1974], p. 141.) Likewise, Harrell R. Rodgers, Jr., in his study of North Carolina schoolchildren, developed a five-item political cynicism index. (See "Toward Explanation of Political Efficacy and Political Cynicism of Black Adolescents: An Exploratory Study," *American Journal of Political Science,* 18 [May 1974], pp. 257–282.) But, in his study with George Taylor of Charleston, South Carolina, schoolchildren, Rodgers used these same five items to build a political trust index. (See "The Policeman as an Agent of Regime Legitimation," *Midwest Journal of Political Science,* 15 [February 1971], pp. 72–86.)

13. See Arthur H. Miller, "Rejoinder to 'Comment' by Jack Citrin: Political Discontent or Ritualism," *American Political Science Review,* 68 (September 1974), pp. 989–1001, at p. 990.

14. See, in particular, Ada W. Finifter's influential article, "Dimensions of Political Alienation." Using the American data from *The Civic Culture* study,

Finifter empirically identified two major components of political alienation, "political powerlessness" and "perceived political normlessness." Political powerlessness is clearly the opposite of feelings of political effectiveness, and perceived political normlessness has often been viewed as a measure of political cynicism.

For an earlier theoretical work that identifies five dimensions of alienation, see Melvin Seeman, "On the Meaning of Alienation," *American Sociological Review,* 24 (December 1959), pp. 783–791.

15. Gamson, *Power and Discontent,* p. 42.

16. For the most extensive treatment of the concept of political support, see David Easton, *A Systems Analysis of Political Life* (New York: Wiley, 1965), pp. 153–340, and Easton, "A Re-Assessment of the Concept of Political Support," *British Journal of Political Science,* 5 (October 1975), pp. 435–457. See also Easton and Dennis, *Children in the Political System,* pp. 57–64.

17. Miller, "Political Issues and Trust in Government," p. 951.

18. *Ibid.*

19. *Ibid.,* p. 971.

20. Jack Citrin, "Comment: The Political Relevance of Trust in Government," *American Political Science Review,* 68 (September 1974), pp. 973–988, at p. 978. Citrin's argument is based on a careful evaluation of the construct validity of the political trust measure.

21. Miller, "Rejoinder to 'Comment' by Jack Citrin," pp. 990–991.

22. Sears, "Political Socialization," pp. 114–117.

23. Counting the two 1965 Michigan samples as separate studies. The large survey of over 20,000 high school seniors (reported in a personal communication by M. Kent Jennings) was based upon questionnaires distributed in a national sample of high schools. The smaller sample of 1666 seniors was based upon interviews conducted in those same schools (see Langton and Jennings, "Political Socialization and the High School Civics Curriculum"). About 1200 of the seniors interviewed were also included in the questionnaire-based sample, and the results of the two surveys are not independent of each other. The results from both data sets are reported, however, for they demonstrate that similar racial differences were obtained regardless of whether questionnaires or interviews were used, and regardless of whether one relied upon an analysis of individual items or upon multi-item scales.

24. As Ted Tapper notes in his critique of my November 1972 *Journal of Politics* article, "the most noticeable feature of the data is the wide fluctuations in percentage distributions from one study to the next." (See Ted Tapper, *Political Education and Stability: Elite Responses to Political Conflict* [New York: Wiley, 1976], pp. 163–164.) But while such fluctuations are noticeable, they may also be misleading. The surveys were not only conducted at different times and places, but also among children of different ages. The items used vary, and, even where the same items are used, authors may choose different cutting points in presenting their data. Despite these inconsistencies one can evaluate between-race differences for each survey, and can compare these between-race differences over time. Even so, one must be cautious about making inferences from the magnitude of these differences and should focus on their direction.

25. See Merton S. Krause, "Schoolchildren's Attitude Toward Public Authority Figures," Chicago, Institute for Juvenile Research, August, 1972, mimeo, pp. 7–9. Krause's study is the only research report for which I present findings for Spanish-Americans, even though such data were also available in studies by David O. Sears, Christine Bennett Button, and Harold M. Barger. Our basic decision was that there were not yet enough available data to build explanations for the political attitudes of Chicanos. Data for Krause's study were reported, however, because of the special nature of his research report. Krause examined between-group differences for four subgroups by using an analysis of variance technique and reported between-group differences that were significant at the .05 level. His data report cannot be presented accurately unless one includes his statements about all significant subgroup differences.

26. Both Jones and Rodgers argue that the areas they studied were atypical. See James T. Jones, "Political Socialization in a Mid-Western Industrial Community," unpublished Ph.D. dissertation, University of Illinois, 1965, pp. 4–102; Rodgers, "Toward Explanation," pp. 260–261.

27. See Lee H. Ehman, "Political Socialization and the High School Social Studies Curriculum," unpublished Ph.D. dissertation, University of Michigan, 1969. In both years of his panel survey, Ehman also conducted a comparison sample of students who were not part of his panel. In Appendix A, I report data only for his panel survey.

28. See Langton and Jennings, "Political Socialization and the High School Civics Curriculum," p. 861; Sandra J. Kenyon, "The Development of Political Cynicism among Negro and White Adolescents," paper presented at 65th Annual Meeting of American Political Science Association, New York, September 1969, p. 18; Schley R. Lyons, "The Political Socialization of Ghetto Children: Efficacy and Cynicism," *Journal of Politics,* 32 (May 1970), pp. 288–304, at pp. 295–296; Alden J. Stevens, "Children's Acquisition of Regime Norms in Subcultures of Race and Social Class: The Problem of System Maintenance," unpublished Ph.D. dissertation, University of Maryland, 1969, pp. 66–69; and William E. Hulbary, "Adolescent Political Self-Images and Political Involvement: The Relative Effects of High School Black Studies Courses and Prior Socialization," unpublished Ph.D. dissertation, University of Iowa, 1972, pp. 50–64.

29. Funderburk, and Jaros and Kolson specifically argue that their samples were atypical. See Samuel C. Funderburk, "Orientations Toward Political Protest and Violence among Children and Adolescents," unpublished Ph.D. dissertation, University of Iowa, 1973, pp. 35–36; Dean Jaros and Kenneth L. Kolson, "The Multifarious Leader; Political Socialization of Amish, 'Yanks,' Blacks," in *The Politics of Future Citizens: New Dimensions in the Political Socialization of Children,* ed. Richard G. Niemi (San Francisco: Jossey-Bass, 1974), pp. 41–62, at pp. 45–46.

30. See Edward S. Greenberg, "Political Socialization to Support of the System: A Comparison of Black and White Children," unpublished Ph.D. dissertation, University of Wisconsin, 1969, p. 296; Lyons, "The Political Socialization of Ghetto Children," pp. 295–297; and Anthony M. Orum and Roberta S. Cohen, "The Development of Political Orientations Among Black

and White Children," *American Sociological Review,* 38 (February 1973), pp. 62–74, at p. 66. In addition, in his personal communication to me, Bruce A. Campbell reported that racial differences persisted after controls for socioeconomic level were introduced.

31. Findings for the first wave of the study are reported in Jerald G. Bachman, *Youth in Transition, Volume 2: The Impact of Family Background and Intelligence on Tenth-Grade Boys* (Ann Arbor, Mich.: Institute for Social Research, 1970), pp. 153–154. The data in Appendix A are based upon a personal communication from Bachman.

32. There are two plausible explanations for the marked decline in political trust among the boys in Bachman's panel. As they aged and gained more experience with politics, they may have become more cynical. But the decline may also result from political conditions that caused these boys to perceive the government as less trustworthy. Indeed, as is well known, there was a marked decline in political trust among American adults during the period in which Bachman's panel was conducted. Here we are not concerned with the overall decline in political trust, but in explaining why trust declined faster for blacks than for whites.

33. Both these surveys were carried out through the Survey Research Center of the University of Michigan.

34. Lee H. Ehman's panel survey is based upon substantially smaller NS than Bachman's, and is drawn from a single high school. His data do not fit the overall trend because he found blacks to be less trusting than whites in a survey conducted before the summer of 1967. By the time of Ehman's second wave trust had declined among both races, but it had fallen much more among blacks than among whites, and blacks had become much less trusting than whites (see Appendix A).

Chapter 2.   Evaluation of the Findings

How reliable are these findings? Can we safely extrapolate from them to the universe of black and white schoolchildren? The sources cited differ greatly in the skill with which the research was reported, and those studies reporting careful multivariate analyses were usually more helpful in our attempts to build explanations. But for our immediate purposes the representativeness of the samples and the reliability and validity of the measures are more important than the quality of the research report.

SAMPLING PROBLEMS

Obviously, we can be most confident of those surveys based upon national probability samples. Thus the Bachman panel and the two Jennings surveys clearly provide the most representative data sets. Jennings' surveys do not include children of twelfth-grade age who are no longer in school and, as blacks of this age are more likely to have left school than whites, the data on blacks are less representative than those on whites. On balance, Bachman's data may be the most representative—at least, of males—for he was able to sample children who were no longer in school, but only if they were in the tenth grade when his panel began.

Both Jennings' data and the Bachman panel are based upon samples of schools, not the universe of adolescents. This poses two problems. First, some schools refused to cooperate, and thus we have samples of children attending schools with authorities willing to allow access to social science researchers. Second, because children of some subgroups, such as blacks, may be found in a relatively small number of schools, samples of such minority groups may not adequately represent the total minority group population.

All other studies are based upon special purpose samples, usually

chosen by the researcher for reasons of convenience. Among the special
purpose samples, those of Marjorie Randon Hershey and Schley R.
Lyons stand out. Hershey's study was based upon a probability sample
of Florida public schools, and although Lyons' sample is based upon
children in a single city (Toledo, Ohio), he systematically dif-
ferentiated between children in inner-city schools and those in schools
outside the inner city. Other studies, such as those by Henry I. Penfield, Jr., Thomas J. Williams, William E. Hulbary, Anthony M. Orum
and Roberta S. Cohen, Samuel Long (in his 1972 sample), and Lorn S.
Foster, have the virtue of sampling from a variety of areas throughout
the state or states they studied. Several authors—in particular, James
T. Jones, Harrell R. Rodgers, Jr., Samuel C. Funderburk, and Dean
Jaros and Kenneth L. Kolson—emphasize that the area they studied
was atypical. Clearly, the most atypical sample is Richard C. Remy's
study of high school seniors from all 50 states who had attended a
nongovernmental educational program in Washington, D.C., during
the Winter of 1971.

Even though most of the samples do not represent the entire nation,
we have collectively reported data from most areas of the United States
and from urban, suburban, and rural school districts. As the map in
Appendix B clearly illustrates, most special purpose samples were conducted in the South and in north central states, but, as of 1970, 53 per
cent and 20 per cent of the nation's blacks lived in these two regions,
respectively.[1] The diverse nature of these research sites does not allow
us to estimate how great the racial differences in political attitudes
would have been if we relied exclusively on national probability samples, but the wide range of sites does give us some confidence that
racial differences discovered by these researchers did not result from
biased sampling from a handful of geographically concentrated school
districts. Clearly, there are racial differences in feelings of political
efficacy and trust; but the actual size of these differences cannot be
estimated from these special purpose samples.

The only systematic bias is that all these researchers, including
those who used probability sampling techniques, depended upon the
cooperation of school officials. With both the Bachman and Jennings
surveys, over 80 per cent of the schools initially selected to be sampled
ultimately cooperated. There is still the possibility that the very
characteristics contributing to school officials refusing entrée to social
scientists might be systematically related to the attitudes of children in those schools. This possibility cannot be tested, except perhaps
by an extremely expensive research design that sampled from the universe of schoolchildren, and in which children were interviewed outside the schools. Nonetheless, we have no reason to believe that schools

that could not be entered housed blacks with high levels of political efficacy and trust, or that they housed whites with low levels. Thus, it seems likely that our conclusion that blacks score lower on these measures would still stand even if we had a more representative sample of the preadult population.

MEASUREMENT PROBLEMS

If we are willing to grant the adequacy of the sampling, we must still ask whether these surveys actually measured feelings of political efficacy and political trust. Have these authors developed reliable and valid measures? Some of these authors rely solely upon the analysis of individual items, whereas others have built indices or developed scales. For our initial purposes presenting racial differences according to individual items is adequate, and gives us a more detailed picture. Given the possible multidimensional character of the concept of political efficacy, we may be better able to trace change over time by examining responses to each efficacy item separately.[2] Unfortunately, the researchers who relied upon an analysis of individual items usually presented less detailed analyses of their data, while those who built indices and scales were more likely to employ multivariate analyses that contribute to building explanations.

The main advantages of using cumulative measures, such as indices and scales, is that they presumably increase measurement reliability and allow one to analyze one's data in a parsimonious way.[3] An index is constructed by adding up scores assigned to individual items, while a scale is built by assigning scores according to the response pattern among the individual items.[4] In fact, this distinction is rarely made in practice. For the most part, researchers who built indices did merely add up the results of the individual items, but they usually used no technique to justify their implicit assumption that these items measured a single dimension. For example, several researchers relied upon David Easton and Jack Dennis' report that factor analytic techniques justify building a cumulative measure of sense of political efficacy. But the unidimensionality of such items should be demonstrated for each sample with which they are applied.[5] By and large, we can be more confident of those measures based upon some type of scaling procedure that demonstrates that the questions used to build a scale measure the same attitudinal dimension. Even so, it should be recognized that many of these researchers applied fairly weak tests to demonstrate the unidimensionality of their measures. Many relied on the coefficient of reproductibility, even though an "acceptable" CR is only a minimal indicator of scale reliability.[6] (Appendix C describes the procedures used by researchers to build indices and scales.)

Whether these items can be used to measure attitudes among blacks is a separate question. Pauline Marie Vaillancourt demonstrated that black schoolchildren tend to have less stable attitudes across time than white children have. Her study was based upon a three-wave panel conducted in the San Francisco Bay area in late 1968 and early 1969, and included 1001 children in the fourth, sixth, and eighth grades.[7] Not only did she find blacks to have less stable responses to attitudinal items, they were also less stable on items purporting to describe demographic and social characteristics, such as age, father's occupation, and religion.[8] But the instability of responses between panels can reflect actual attitude change, and the least stable questions in Vaillancourt's panel, those measuring images of the president, clearly reflect systematic responses to Richard Nixon replacing Johnson.[9] Moreover, even if *individual* attitudes are unstable over time, mean differences between *groups* can be reliably measured.

Some black scholars, in personal communications to me, reject the notion that these items, originally designed to measure attitudes for the overall population, can measure feelings among blacks. They argue that these items may not have the same meaning for blacks as they have for whites. But it seems unwise to reject this extensive body of research on the chance that these items do not tap black political attitudes. Admittedly, we would have more confidence if researchers had demonstrated that the items that can be used to build scales for their overall sample could also be used to build scales for the black subset of their sample. Nonetheless, these items do seem to have considerable face validity (an admittedly weak test), and we have some evidence that they do measure the same attitudes among blacks as among whites.[10]

Racial differences on feelings of political efficacy and trust were usually not large, but in most cases we can reject the null hypothesis that racial differences are likely to result from chance. These findings can be accepted as phenomena to be explained because, first, surveys based upon national probability samples support them; and second, and perhaps equally important, the consistency among findings from separate studies is high. Twenty of 30 surveys show blacks to feel less politically efficacious than whites, regardless of the items used, and five of the remaining surveys provide some evidence that blacks feel less efficacious; 24 of the 33 surveys conducted during and after the summer of 1967 found blacks to be less politically trusting than whites, and four of the remaining surveys also provided some evidence that they were less trusting. The collective weight of evidence provided by

these separate surveys provides a strong reason for developing explanations for these findings.

NOTES

1. U.S. Bureau of the Census, *Statistical Abstract of the United States:
1972*, 93d ed. (Washington, D.C.: U.S. Government Printing Office, 1972),
p. 26.

2. As Philip E. Converse notes, the items used to measure feelings of political effectiveness among adults (which are similar to those used to measure
these feelings among children) have followed different trend lines since the
1950s. For three items there has been a decline in efficacy, while more respondents now disagree that voting is the only way people can influence the government. "This is an interesting case," Converse writes, "of a scale deemed
unidimensional by Guttman criteria in 1952, one component of which has
pulled out of line rather markedly in response to phenotypic events in a subsequent period. Our analysis of these trends would have been greatly muddied
if we had proceeded with the composite scale taken as a whole." Philip E.
Converse, "Change in the American Electorate," in *The Human Meaning of
Social Change,* eds. Angus Campbell and Philip E. Converse (New York: Russell Sage, 1972), pp. 263–337, at p. 329.

3. For a discussion of the advantages of multiple-item measures, see Jum
C. Nunnally,*Psychometric Theory* (New York: McGraw-Hill, 1967), pp. 56–58.

4. For a discussion of the differences between an index and a scale, see Earl
R. Babbie, *Survey Research Methods* (Belmont, Calif.: Wadsworth, 1973), pp.
253–278.

5. For example, Harrell R. Rodgers, Jr., conducted a factor analysis to
determine the unidimensionality of the five items frequently used to measure
feelings of political effectiveness among preadults. He found that, with his
North Carolina sample, only three items could be used for his index. See
Harrell R. Rodgers, Jr., "Toward Explanation of the Political Efficacy and
Political Cynicism of Black Adolescents: An Exploratory Study," *American
Journal of Political Science,* 18 (May 1974), pp. 257–282, at pp. 261–262.

6. For a discussion of problems in building acceptable Guttman scales, see
Nunnally, *Psychometric Theory,* pp. 63–66, and R. J. Mokken, *A Theory and
Procedure of Scale Analysis with Applications in Political Research* (The
Hague: Mouton, 1971), pp. 23–71.

7. Vaillancourt's data on racial differences in feelings of political effectiveness are based upon a subset of children sampled in the last wave of her panel.
Her findings about trust are based upon that portion of her panel which was
asked the closed-ended questions about the president.

8. See Pauline Marie Vaillancourt, "The Stability of Children's Political
Orientations: A Panel Study," paper presented at 66th Annual Meeting of
American Political Science Association, Los Angeles, September 1970, pp.

21–22. See also Vaillancourt, "Stability of Children's Survey Responses," *Public Opinion Quarterly,* 37 (Fall 1973), pp. 373–387, at pp. 380–381.

9. See pp. 86–87.

10. Herbert Jacob argues that scales used to measure feeling of political efficacy among whites should not be used to measure feelings of efficacy among blacks unless one demonstrates that such scales are reliable measures for the black subsample. He concludes, "It is fallacious to assert—on the basis of such scales—that blacks are less efficacious than whites, because the scale may not measure the same thing among blacks and whites." ("Problems of Scale Equivalency in Measuring Attitudes in American Subcultures," *Social Science Quarterly,* 52 [June 1971], pp. 61–75, at p. 62.)

But Jacob's analysis of the Michigan SRC samples showed that the reliability of the SRC sense of political efficacy scale was slightly higher among blacks than among whites in 1952, while being slightly lower in 1956 and 1968. Data from a Milwaukee sample also showed only negligible differences between blacks and whites in the reliability of both the political efficacy scale and the Jennings-Niemi political cynicism scale. Only a statewide Wisconsin survey, in which only 19 blacks were sampled, showed blacks to have a different attitude structure than whites had with the political efficacy items. The bulk of Jacob's evidence actually suggests that one may validly use standard political efficacy items when studying black attitudes.

A careful analysis of the 1968 and 1970 SRC surveys by James D. Wright also suggests that the SRC efficacy items are about as reliable for black adults as for white adults. The standard trust items yielded somewhat lower inter-item correlations for blacks than for whites, but Wright argues that these items may *underestimate* black discontent. (See James D. Wright, *The Dissent of the Governed: Alienation and Democracy in America* [New York: Academic Press, 1976], pp. 92–95.)

PART II

Explanations

INTRODUCTION

Why do black schoolchildren feel politically less efficacious and trusting than white children do? If we were attempting to explain racial differences in these attitudes among adults our task might be simpler, for adults have much more political experience and knowledge than children, and we might move directly to the political-reality explanation. But our task is complicated because children, unlike adults, are all politically powerless. Of course, racial differences among schoolchildren might result from racial differences among adults, but we have almost no data that directly support the thesis that children learn attitudes such as feelings of political efficacy and trust from adults.

Our task is further complicated because few studies that report racial differences in political attitudes attempt to explain them. Most authors are content merely to report their findings. This is unfortunate, for those studies that do attempt to develop explanations often lead to multivariate analyses that can be used to test our explanations. Often a rich data analysis contributes to testing explanations that the original authors did not directly consider. However, the authors who did not test explanations should not be criticized too severely. Some were not exploring for racial differences, and merely reported their results by race because such reports are socially interesting. Other authors at least advanced explanations for racial differences in these attitudes. Schley R. Lyons, for example, briefly advanced a social-

24

psychological explanation for low feelings of political efficacy among black schoolchildren, and Edward S. Greenberg offered an explanation for low trust that is similar to our political-reality explanation. Both Lyons and Greenberg provided partial tests of their explanations, but their tests were weak because they neither advanced nor tested other plausible explanations for racial differences. Joan E. Laurence argued that low black efficacy and trust resulted from the political realities faced by black Americans, but she did not test her thesis. Anthony M. Orum and Roberta S. Cohen briefly offered two explanations for low political trust among black schoolchildren, a "psychodynamic" explanation and a "subcultural" one, and provided a preliminary test of both. The most extensive tests of explanations, however, are provided by Harrell R. Rodgers, Jr., and by Samuel Long, and their tests will be discussed at length at the end of each relevant chapter.

At least four possible explanations might account for racial differences in feelings of political efficacy and trust among schoolchildren. They are:

A. Racial differences result from differences in political education within American schools—the *political-education* explanation.
B. Racial differences result from social-structural conditions that contribute to low feelings of self-confidence among blacks—the *social-deprivation* explanation.
C. Racial differences result from differences in intelligence—the *intelligence* explanation.
D. Racial differences result from differences in the political environment in which blacks and whites live—the *political-reality* explanation.

Each explanation will be discussed in a separate chapter, and each chapter will follow the same structure. We will begin by examining the assumptions that constitute the explanation, and evaluating the theoretical and empirical support for each assumption. Next, we will consider additional empirical relations that would follow if the explanation were valid, and we will label these additional empirical consequences. We will determine whether extant socialization research has discovered the relationships predicted by those consequences. Next we will examine discussions and tests of earlier formulations of the explanation. Last, we will evaluate the explanation. In Chapter 7 we will evaluate them comparatively, spelling out the theoretical and research consequences of extant socialization research about black Americans.

Before beginning our discussion, two points must be stressed. First, we are not arguing that these explanations are actually valid, only that they deserve preliminary consideration given our knowledge about the political socialization process. We will find, for example, that there is weak theoretical and little empirical support for the intelligence explanation. Second, these explanations are not mutually exclusive. In principle, these explanations could be mutually exclusive, but in the actual world of American society and politics the circumstances out of which they arise are not. More than one of these explanations could constitute a valid partial explanation for the low feelings of political efficacy and trust among black preadults.

To help the reader follow the discussion, the basic assumptions of each explanation, and the empirical consequences that follow from each, are listed in Appendix D.

Chapter 3.   The Political-Education Explanation

American schools explicitly teach political values through the formal content of the curriculum. But teachers may also stress political values implicitly. Black children probably are not taught that they have little ability to influence political leaders, but they may be indirectly taught not to participate actively in politics.

The following assumptions constitute the political-education explanation:

Assumption A.1. Students learn the political values taught in the schools. In other words, the schools are effective agents of political socialization.

Assumption A.2. Teachers are less likely to stress norms of political participation when teaching black children than when teaching white children.

Each of these assumptions can be questioned.

Assumption A.1. Unless children learn the political values taught in the schools, differences in political education cannot contribute to racial differences in political values. American schools attempt to teach political values, but we have no compelling evidence that children learn them. Unlike mathematics or physics, which are learned almost exclusively in the schools, children learn about politics from many sources; thus the effectiveness of the school as a political socialization agent is weakened. In fact, there is little direct evidence that the schools succeed in teaching political values.

The strongest argument for the power of the school as an agent of political socialization was advanced by Robert D. Hess and Judith V. Torney, who discovered that siblings were not likely to have identical political values, except for partisanship. They concluded that "the school apparently plays the largest part in teaching attitudes, conceptions, and beliefs about the operation of the political system."[1] In their analysis of the 1965 SRC study of high school seniors, M. Kent Jennings and Richard G. Niemi directly compared the attitudes of high school seniors and their parents.[2] They found that on a majority of issues seniors were unlikely to have the same political values as their parents and concluded that the school might be playing a greater role in the political socialization process than had previously been believed. For example, they speculated that the low levels of political cynicism found among high school seniors (in 1965) might result from values taught in schools. But both these conclusions are based entirely upon indirect evidence that the family fails to transmit political attitudes, not upon direct evidence that students learn the values taught in the classroom.

Jennings, along with Kenneth P. Langton, also used the 1965 SRC data to evaluate the impact of civics courses.[3] However, their basic approach was to compare students who had taken civics courses with those who had not, and they did not examine the values taught in those courses. As a result their findings, though quite interesting, cannot be used as a test of Assumption A.1.[4]

The assumption that students learn the political values taught in the schools is not supported by extant research. But neither does available research allow us to reject this assumption.

Assumption A.2. Even if we accept the assumption that schools are effective agents of political socialization, the political-education explanation cannot be valid unless blacks and whites are taught different values. Are teachers less likely to stress the norms of political participation when teaching black children than when teaching white children? We can advance sound reasons for expecting this to be the case. A large percentage of blacks live either in the South or in ghettos in Northern cities, and in most of these settings school authorities are white. Such schools may not emphasize the norm of political participation. Since white teachers probably do not see blacks as future social and political leaders, they may subtly teach them that political participation is inappropriate. In the South black teachers may be reluctant to teach participatory norms.[5]

Few studies, however, demonstrate that blacks are taught to be political nonparticipants. After observing schools in two North Carolina cities, Bradbury Seasholes concluded that blacks in Southern schools are taught the "norm" of nonparticipation.[6] Several impressionistic studies of black education indirectly support the assumption that blacks are taught nonparticipation.[7] One of the most suggestive studies of educational differences in American schools was by Edgar Litt, who found sharp differences between working- and middle-class schools in the Boston area.[8] Teachers in middle-class schools stressed the norms of political participation, while those in working-class schools emphasized obedience. But Litt's study did not present data according to racial differences.

A related approach might argue that the "educational climate" in schools that blacks attend tends to differ from the climate in schools attended by whites.[9] Lee H. Ehman and Judith A. Gillespie argue that while most schools have bureaucratic "political climates," in which channels of participation run from the administration down to the teachers and students, some have relatively participatory authority patterns allowing students and teachers to influence decisions.[10] Schools with participatory patterns, they argue, should encourage feelings of political competence. While Ehman and Gillespie present no extensive argument to support this hypothesis, it seems consistent with Gabriel A. Almond and Sidney Verba's finding that adults who said they had been consulted about school decisions tended to have higher feelings of political competence than those who said they had not been consulted.[11] Ehman and Gillespie do show that feelings of political competence were somewhat higher among children attending the one school that had a relatively participatory political climate.[12] But they provide no discussion of racial differences among different types of schools. Before the school climate argument could be used to support Assumption A.2, we would need to (a) spell out those "climatic" conditions that contribute to feelings of political effectiveness (and trust), and (b) demonstrate empirically that blacks attend schools lacking those conditions.[13]

At present we have little evidence to support the assumption that blacks are taught different political values than whites are, but neither do we have data that allow us to reject this assumption. If, however, we provisionally accept both assumptions of the political-education explanation, we can predict additional empirical relationships that could be tested if appropriate data were available. I call such predictions additional empirical consequences. The political-education explanation leads to one such consequence:

Empirical Consequence A.1. Black children should be less likely to have a participatory view of the polity and their role within the polity than white children have.

Kenneth P. Langton and M. Kent Jennings found that whites were more likely than blacks to stress participatory norms when defining the role of the good citizen, while blacks were more likely than whites to stress loyalty.[14] Joan E. Laurence found that black schoolchildren were less likely to participate in politics than white children were.[15] Edward S. Greenberg's research suggests that black schoolchildren were more likely than whites to have a "subject," rather than a "participant," orientation toward American politics, and that these dif-

ferences were not the spurious result of social class.[16] Alden J. Stevens
found that blacks scored much lower than whites on a "political duty"
scale and concluded, "Children in the black subculture do not appear to
generally learn attitudes which stimulate participation."[17] Pauline
Marie Vaillancourt found that black schoolchildren were less likely to
discuss politics than white children were.[18] Thomas J. Williams reports that blacks were less likely to choose "voting" as a symbol of
government than whites were.[19] Referring to an earlier formulation
of my explanation,[20] Williams proceeds to argue that this failure to
select voting may result from political education, and concludes that
the political-education explanation "might be more plausible than Abramson supposes."[21] Most of the blacks surveyed by Williams were in
all-black schools with black teachers. "It could very well be," he writes,
"that these instructors did not emphasize this norm [voting] as much
as white instructors because of their perception of the realities of
Southern politics and/or because of their own personal sense of ineffectiveness."[22]

But not all studies show blacks to score low on participatory norms.
Jack Dennis, for example, found that among eleventh graders blacks
were somewhat more likely than whites to emphasize participatory
aspects of democracy, and were as likely as whites to mention political
participation as an attribute of good citizenship.[23] Vaillancourt found
that blacks scored somewhat higher than whites on an index of political
participation.[24] And Anthony M. Orum and Roberta S. Cohen found
that black children were more likely to discuss politics than white children were, and were somewhat more likely to score high on an index of
political participation.[25] Harrell R. Rodgers, Jr., also failed to find
support for Empirical Consequence A.1, but before we discuss his findings we will place his discussion in its total context, a systematic attempt to test all four explanations.

HARRELL R. RODGERS, JR.'S TEST OF THE
POLITICAL-EDUCATION EXPLANATION

Rodgers has conducted a conscientious and well-reasoned test of all
four of my explanations, as they were advanced in my paper of May
1971.[26] In addition, he tests an "environmental politicization" explanation developed by Kenneth P. Langton and David A. Karns. In many
respects, Rodgers' article is a model of cogent data analysis applied to
theory building. However, two basic problems limited his efforts.

In the first place, Rodgers' survey of Edgecombe County, North
Carolina, high school students was conducted before my paper was

written. Since his survey instrument was extraordinarily rich, he was able to conduct many innovative tests. Nonetheless, many of his indicators did not directly measure the variables suggested by my explanations. He acknowledges that "our data are frequently not adequate for a thorough evaluation of each explanation," but maintains that a partial test can be conducted for all the explanations. "The analysis," he argues, "could have been restricted to only those explanations for which complete data were available, but in this basically unexplored area we thought the most complete analysis possible was desirable."[27] Rodgers' basic research decision was fundamentally sound, but in some cases he could conduct only partial and incomplete tests of the explanations.

Rodgers confronted a second problem. His sample was one of the few in which blacks felt marginally more efficacious and trusting than whites.[28] Racial differences in efficacy and trust were negligible because the whites in Rodgers' sample had far lower feelings of political efficacy and trust than those in most other surveys.[29] The absence of racial differences in these attitudes poses a basic analytical problem. The best way to test these explanations is by introducing relevant controls that might eliminate or reduce racial differences in feelings of efficacy and trust. For example, if the low feelings of political efficacy and trust among blacks result from social deprivation, racial differences in those feelings should be nonexistent, or at least smaller, among blacks and whites at comparable levels of deprivation. But when attitudinal differences do not exist, or if blacks feel more efficacious and trusting than whites, the logic of this analysis is greatly confounded.[30] Rodgers chose not to examine the antecedents of political efficacy and trust among whites (although logically they are the same as those for blacks). Rather, he focused on explaining variation in feelings of political efficacy and trust among blacks.

Rodgers began by examining the political-education explanation. He could not test this explanation directly, for to do so one needs to know the content of political education within the schools. As Rodgers did not have data about the values taught in the schools, he could not determine whether such values were learned. Most important, he did not determine whether teachers in Edgecombe County were less likely to stress the norms of political participation when teaching blacks than when teaching whites.

Rodgers correctly notes that the political-education explanation focuses exclusively on the low political efficacy among black children, and does not attempt to account for their low political trust. In fact, Rodgers argues that the explanation might predict black children to have high levels of trust, for "if they [blacks] are taught obedience they would probably be taught loyalty at the same time."[31] In fact, blacks in his sample did have slightly lower levels of political cynicism than whites. Yet he argues that the blacks he sampled were more cynical than Northern whites, and also as cynical as Northern blacks,[32] findings that lead him to question the veracity of the political-education explanation.

Rodgers was able to test directly Empirical Consequence A.1, that black children should be less likely to have a participatory view of the polity and their role within the polity than white children have. He found no support for this proposition. Students were asked whether they expected to be active in politics when they grew up, and black students expected to be active more often than white students did. Moreover, when students were asked to describe the characteristics of the "good citizen," blacks were no more likely than whites to emphasize loyalty over participation. Thus, Rodgers concluded, "It is probably safe to reject the education explanation for this sample."[33]

EVALUATION OF THE POLITICAL-EDUCATION EXPLANATION

Although we cannot empirically support its assumptions, the political-education explanation is, in principle, capable of accounting for the low feelings of political efficacy among black schoolchildren. Can it also explain their low feelings of political trust? If blacks are taught to be politically passive, they are probably also taught to revere political authorities. There could be some settings, for example, where the teacher is a black militant, where blacks were taught to feel powerless to influence political leaders through conventional channels, but were also taught to distrust political authorities. But in most schools we would not expect blacks to be taught to distrust political leaders. At best, then, the political-education explanation is silent about Finding 2.

NOTES

1. Robert D. Hess and Judith V. Torney, *The Development of Political Attitudes in Children* (Chicago: Aldine, 1967), p. 217.

2. M. Kent Jennings and Richard G. Niemi, "The Transmission of Political Attitudes from Parent to Child," *American Political Science Review,* 62 (March 1968), pp. 169–184.

3. Kenneth P. Langton and M. Kent Jennings, "Political Socialization and

the High School Civics Curriculum in the United States," *American Political Science Review,* 62 (September 1968), pp. 852–867.

4. However, we will later compare the Langton and Jennings results with those obtained by Harrell R. Rodgers, Jr., in his test of the political-reality explanation. See p. 104.

5. Donald R. Matthews and James W. Prothro, for example, argued that Southern black professionals with college educations often had relatively low levels of political participation, because their jobs depended so directly upon the white community. (See *Negroes and the New Southern Politics* [New York: Harcourt, Brace, and World, 1966], pp. 85–86.) This may, of course, be less true in the mid-1970s than in 1961 when Matthews and Prothro conducted their interviews.

6. Bradbury Seasholes, "Negro Political Participation in Two North Carolina Cities," unpublished Ph.D. dissertation, University of North Carolina, 1962.

7. See, for example, Jonathan Kozol, *Death at an Early Age: The Destruction of the Hearts and Minds of Negro Children in the Boston Public Schools* (New York: Bantam Books, 1967); Eleanor Burke Leacock, *Teaching and Learning in City Schools: A Comparative Study* (New York: Basic Books, 1969); and Kenneth B. Clark, *Dark Ghetto: Dilemmas of Social Power* (New York: Harper and Row, 1965), pp. 111–153.

8. Edgar Litt, "Civic Education, Community Norms, and Political Indoctrination," *American Sociological Review,* 28 (February 1963), pp. 69–75.

9. For a discussion of this concept, see Martin L. Levin, "Social Climates and Political Socialization," *Public Opinion Quarterly,* 25 (Winter 1961), pp. 596–606; and Richard M. Merelman, *Political Socialization and Educational Climates: A Study of Two School Districts* (New York: Holt, Rinehart, and Winston, 1971).

10. Lee H. Ehman and Judith A. Gillespie, "Political Life in the Hidden Curriculum: Does it Make a Difference?," paper presented at 54th Annual Meeting of National Council of the Social Studies, Chicago, November 1974.

11. Garbiel A. Almond and Sidney Verba, *The Civic Culture: Political Attitudes and Democracy in Five Nations* (Princeton, N.J.: Princeton University Press, 1963), pp. 352–361.

12. Ehman and Gillespie, "Political Life in the Hidden Curriculum," p. 46.

13. We have little systematic data about the political climate of schools attended by blacks. However, Richard C. Remy's survey of high school seniors reported in Appendix A suggests that black students may have less opportunity to participate within the school decision-making process than white students have. The study, based upon students selected to attend a nongovernmental training program in Washington, D.C., in the winter of 1971, was based predominantly upon college-bound, middle-class students. Only 14 per cent of these students felt powerless about the decision-making process within their schools. However, black students tended to have a higher sense of powerlessness than white students had. See D. John Grove, Richard C. Remy, and L. Harmon Zeigler, "The Effects of Political Ideology and Educational

Climates on Student Dissent," *American Politics Quarterly,* 2 (July 1974), pp. 259–275, at p. 267.

14. Langton and Jennings, "Political Socialization and the High School Civics Curriculum," pp. 863–864.

15. Joan E. Laurence, "White Socialization: Black Reality," *Psychiatry,* 33 (May 1970), pp. 174–194, at p. 180. Laurence measured nine forms of political activity, including writing a letter to the president, helping a candidate, talking about a candidate, and reading about politics.

16. Edward S. Greenberg, "Political Socialization to Support of the System: A Comparison of Black and White Children," unpublished Ph.D. dissertation, University of Wisconsin, 1969, pp. 155–162; and Greenberg, "Children and Government: A Comparison Across Racial Lines," *Midwest Journal of Political Science,* 14 (May 1970), pp. 249–275, at pp. 267–273.

17. Alden J. Stevens, "Children's Acquisition of Regime Norms in Subcultures of Race and Social Class: The Problem of System Maintenance," unpublished Ph.D. dissertation, University of Maryland, 1969, p. 59.

18. Pauline Marie Vaillancourt, "The Political Socialization of Young People: A Panel Survey of Youngsters in the San Francisco Bay Area," unpublished Ph.D. dissertation, University of California, Berkeley, 1972, p. 332.

19. Thomas J. Williams, "Subcultural Differences in Political Socialization among Selected Children in Georgia," unpublished Ph.D. dissertation, University of Georgia, 1972, pp. 223–229.

20. Williams was discussing an early version of my paper, "Political Efficacy and Political Trust among Black Schoolchildren: Four Alternative Explanations," paper presented at Conference on Political Theory and Political Education, Michigan State University, February 1971.

21. Williams, "Subcultural Differences in Political Socialization," p. 261.

22. *Ibid.,* pp. 261–262.

23. Jack Dennis, *Political Learning in Childhood and Adolescence: A Study of Fifth, Eighth, and Eleventh Graders in Milwaukee, Wisconsin* (Madison: Wisconsin Research and Development Center for Cognitive Learning, 1969), pp. 34–35.

24. Vaillancourt, "The Political Socialization of Young People," p. 332. Based upon a three-item political participation measure, including wearing a campaign button, helping a candidate, and reading about a candidate.

25. Anthony M. Orum and Roberta S. Cohen, "The Development of Political Orientations among Black and White Children," *American Sociological Review,* 38 (February 1973), pp. 62–74, at pp. 67–88. Based upon a three-item discussion measure, including talking with friends, teachers, and parents, and a three-item participation measure, including wearing a campaign button, helping a candidate, and taking part in a demonstration.

26. See Harrell R. Rodgers, Jr., "Toward Explanation of the Political Efficacy and Political Cynicism of Black Adolescents: An Exploratory Study," *American Journal of Political Science,* 18 (May 1974), pp. 257–282. Rodgers' test was based upon the explanations as advanced in my paper, "Political Efficacy and Political Trust among Black Schoolchildren: Four Explanations,"

revised version of paper presented at Conference on Political Theory and Political Education, Michigan State University. (Revised paper dated May 1971.)

27. Rodgers, "Toward Explanation," p. 266.

28. Rodgers did find that blacks were less likely than whites to trust the police (see Appendix A). However, his test of the explanations correctly focused on his five-item measure of political cynicism that taps more generalized feelings about trust than the single item about the police.

29. Rodgers, "Toward Explanation," pp. 262–263. Rodgers directly compared the whites in his Edgecombe County sample with whites sampled by Schley R. Lyons in his study of Toledo schoolchildren. (See Lyons, "The Political Socialization of Ghetto Children: Efficacy and Cynicism," *Journal of Politics,* 32 [May 1970], pp. 288–304.) Although comparisons are difficult, it would appear that the whites sampled by Rodgers had low feelings of political efficacy and trust compared with whites of the same age sampled in most other surveys.

30. If blacks felt as politically efficacious and trusting as whites, even when they were socially deprived compared with whites, the explanation suggests that blacks would feel more efficacious and trusting than whites once controls for levels of social deprivation were introduced.

In the above hypothetical example, the social deprivation of blacks would "suppress" their true *higher* feelings of political efficacy and trust. Unfortunately, there are few empirical analyses that attempt to examine the effects of suppressor variables. For one example, which uses feelings of political competence as the dependent variable, see Ada W. Finifter and Paul R. Abramson, "City Size and Feelings of Political Competence," *Public Opinion Quarterly,* 39 (Summer 1975), pp. 189–198. See also Morris Rosenberg, "The Logical Status of Suppressor Variables," *Public Opinion Quarterly,* 37 (Fall 1973), pp. 359–372.

31. Rodgers, "Toward Explanation," pp. 266–267.

32. *Ibid.,* p. 267. Again, Rodgers' comparison was with Lyons' Toledo sample. However, Rodgers' survey was conducted nearly a year after Lyons', and during this period there was a marked decline in trust among black Americans.

33. *Ibid.*

Chapter 4.   The Social-Deprivation Explanation

The social-deprivation explanation can be summarized as follows. Social deprivation contributes to low feelings of self-confidence and, in particular, to feelings that one cannot control his or her environment. Feelings of personal self-confidence contribute to feelings of political effectiveness and to feelings of political trust. Blacks are socially deprived and their feelings of self-confidence are low. This low self-confidence contributes to low levels of political efficacy and political trust.

Five assumptions constitute the social-deprivation explanation:

Assumption B.1. Persons deprived of opportunity and denied respect tend to have low levels of self-confidence and, in particular, a feeling that they cannot control their social environment.

Assumption B.2. Persons who have low levels of self-confidence tend to have low feelings of political effectiveness.

Assumption B.3. Persons who have low levels of self-confidence tend to have low feelings of political trust.

Assumption B.4. Black children are deprived of opportunity and denied respect.

Assumption B.5. Black children have lower levels of self-confidence than white children have and, in particular, are less likely to feel they can control their social environment.

Although the data are by no means conclusive, there is both some theoretical and empirical support for each of these assumptions.

Assumption B.1. Erik H. Erikson argues that some level of basic trust is essential to feelings of personal adequacy: "The firm establishment of enduring patterns for the solution of the nuclear conflict of basic trust versus basic mistrust in mere existence is the first task of the ego."[1] Trust is not easily maintained, Erikson believes, for the child must eventually be abandoned by his parents. "It is against this powerful combination of a sense of having been deprived, of having been divided, and of having been abandoned—that basic trust must maintain itself throughout life."[2]

M. Brewster Smith presents a different formulation to explain the development of self-confidence. Although Smith acknowledges that basic trust is essential to develop feelings of personal adequacy, he maintains that, given an essential minimum of trust, hope is the more crucial attitude in explaining self-confidence.[3] Smith postulates a set of social-psychological conditions that mutually reinforce feelings of competence. For a self-confident individual, "The self is perceived as causally important, as effective in the world—which is to a major extent a world of other people—as likely to be able to bring about desired effects, and as accepting responsibility when effects do not correspond to desire."[4] This attitude leads to a distinctive world view: "The world is the sort of place in which, given appropriate efforts, I can expect good outcomes. Hope provides the ground against which planning, forbearance, and effort are rational."[5]

Although Smith is concerned primarily with the psychological conditions contributing to self-confidence, he also recognizes ways in which "factors of social structure—especially social class and ghetto status—impinge on the development of competence."

> I think there are such strategic aspects of location in the social structure: *opportunity, respect,* and *power.* . . . Restriction of opportunity not only blights hope; it excludes the person from the chance to acquire the knowledge and skill that would in turn enable him to surmount the barriers to effectiveness. Contempt and withheld respect may lead to "self-hatred" . . . and may necessitate debilitating postures of self-defence. Absence of power entails general vulnerability and creates dependence.[6]

Impressive data document the assumption that persons with restricted opportunities do have low levels of self-confidence.[7] The most impressive single data set was provided by James S. Coleman's comprehensive study of American schoolchildren. Coleman and his colleagues employed three items to measure a child's "sense of control of his environment."[8] They found that children from low-income families were less likely to feel they could control their environment than those with high-income families and that children from homes with the father absent scored lower in sense of control than those from homes where the father was present.[9] The feelings of underprivileged children that they cannot control their environment, Coleman suggests, may result from the actual conditions of deprivation that, in fact, reduce their environmental control:

> One may speculate that these conceptions reasonably derive from the different experiences that these children have had. A child from an advantaged family most often has had all his needs satisfied, has lived in a

responsive environment, and hence can assume that the environment will continue to be responsive if only he acts appropriately. A child from a disadvantaged family has had few of his needs satisfied, has lived in an unresponsive environment, both within the family (where other demands pressed upon his mother) and outside the family, in an outside and often unfriendly world. Thus he cannot assume that the environment will respond to his actions. Such a state of affairs could be expected to lead to passivity, with a general belief in luck, a belief that that world is hostile, and also a belief that nothing he could ever do would change things. He has not yet come to see that he can affect his environment, for it has never been so in his previous experience.[10]

Factors other than social deprivation may also contribute to the development of self-confidence, such as child-rearing patterns and peer-group relationships. But the restriction of social opportunity clearly seems to lower feelings of personal self-confidence and, in particular, the feelings that one can control his or her environment.[11]

Assumption B.2. Persons who have low levels of self-confidence tend to have low feelings of political effectiveness.

If the social-deprivation explanation is valid, the intervening psychological variable, self-confidence, and two dependent variables, sense of political effectiveness and feelings of political trust, must be related. Robert E. Lane argues that personal self-confidence provides a psychological basis for developing feelings of political efficacy. "Men who have feelings of mastery and are endowed with ego strength tend to generalize these sentiments and to feel that their votes are important, politicians respect them, and elections, are, therefore, meaningful processes."[12] We would argue that persons who feel they can control their social environment are more likely to believe they can control their political environment as well.

Several empirical studies document this relationship. Angus Campbell and his colleagues developed a measure of personal effectiveness that tapped "feelings of mastery over the self and the environment."[13] Persons with strong feelings of personal effectiveness were more likely to score high on feelings of political efficacy, and this relationship was not the spurious result of educational differences.[14] Paul M. Sniderman's analysis is particularly important for he differentiates between three types of personal competence: personal unworthiness, interpersonal competence, and status inferiority.[15] By analyzing Herbert McClosky's 1955 "marginal believer" study, and McClosky's 1958 study of political leaders and followers, Sniderman demonstrates that all three aspects of personal competence contribute to high feelings of political competence. Persons with high self-esteem (with all three measures) were more likely to believe that they had a voice in politics, that politicans would pay attention to them, and that they could influence political affairs.[16] "Self-esteem," Sniderman concludes, "taps a person's beliefs about his capacity to cope with the environment. The person with high self-esteem has confidence in himself, in his ability to deal effectively with the problem he confronts, in his chances for success and achievement."[17]

Studies of adolescents also tend to document the relationship between feelings of personal competence and feelings of political effectiveness. Roberta S. Sigel's survey of high school students in rural western New York found that students who believed that environmental rewards and punishments were related directly to their own efforts scored markedly higher on feelings of political effectiveness than those who felt that their own efforts contributed little to outcomes affecting them.[18] Other studies, using a variety of psychological measures, have found that children with strong feelings of personal effectiveness were more likely to feel politically effective than those with low levels of self-confidence, although in some cases these relationships were weak.[19]

Although we would expect personal self-confidence and feelings of political competence to be related, we would not expect all persons who felt personally effective to feel politically effective. An individual with high levels of personal confidence might be uninterested in politics and, as a result of this indifference, politically inefficacious. On the other hand, some persons with low feelings of personal effectiveness might have personal ties to political leaders, and thus feel they can affect political decisions. Indeed, there are data suggesting that feelings of personal competence, as measured by Julian B. Rotter's internal-external scale, are distinct from feelings that the individual citizen can influence political institutions.[20] William F. Stone, a psychologist, reaches sound conclusions: "Expectancies for personal control cannot by themselves explain differences in political activity. One reason for the lack of consistent relationships between internal-external control and participation may lie in differences in knowledge of the opportunities for participation. A person who believes in his own personal effectiveness could conceivably be so unfamiliar with the political system that he feels ineffective in political matters."[21] Stone, whose discussion relies upon the Rotter internal-external distinction, concludes that an individual's entire personality structure should be considered when attempting to explain his or her levels of political participation and feelings of political effectiveness. But the actual social and political situation must also be considered, Stone argues, "since there may be very good reasons why internals are involved at certain times and places, and externals at others."[22]

Assumption B.3. Persons who have low levels of self-confidence tend to have low feelings of political trust.

Erikson's formulation suggests that trust and self-confidence are strongly related. Lane suggests that personal trust, self-confidence, and trust in political leaders are all related: "If one cannot trust other people generally, one can certainly not trust those under the temptations of and with the powers which come with public office. Trust in elected officials is seen to be only a more specific instance of trust in mankind. And in the long run, this is probably a projection of attitudes toward the self—self-approval."[23]

Sniderman extends this line of reasoning, and provides an empirical test.[24] Sniderman writes, "Individuals who think poorly of themselves tend to think poorly of others. They lack confidence in the honesty and amiability of others, and their suspicion, coupled with hostility, invites a deep cynicism about democratic government."[25] And, Sniderman continues, "The person with low self-esteem is also likely to have little confidence in public officials. The hostility and suspiciousness which low self-esteem engenders tend to be pervasive. Thus, the person who thinks little of himself ought to think little of those in public life." Persons with low self-esteem, Sniderman argues, should be more likely "to believe that politicians are people of small ability, untrustworthy, hypocritical, and more intent on serving their own interest than the public welfare."[26] Sniderman's findings support his thesis. Using a combined measure of self-esteem that included all three components of this concept, Sniderman found that persons with low self-esteem were more likely to be politically cynical. They felt that politicans were hypocritical, cared merely about winning elections, and told people what they thought would help them win, and that elected officials did not care what the people think.[27] In addition, persons with low self-esteem were more likely to score high on a political suspiciousness scale that directly measured whether they thought political leaders could be trusted.[28]

More recent data collected by Stanley Allen Renshon also support this reasoning.[29] In his 1971 survey of University of Pennsylvania students, Renshon directly used an adaptation of Rotter's internal-external control scale to build a measure of sense of personal control over the environment, and so, while his sample is less representative than the McClosky data used by Sniderman, his measure more directly bears on our thesis. Using a semantic differential technique, Renshon built a three-item faith-in-government index that directly measured perceptions of governmental honesty. As Renshon writes, "The data suggest that there is a strong relationship between personal control and faith in government. The results are especially striking on the negative evaluation or low faith-in-government category. The overwhelming majority of the respondents with low personal control have little faith in government."[30]

A relationship between low self-confidence and low political trust has also been found among adolescents, although the results have been mixed. Again, Sigel found a strong positive relationship between a belief that one could control his environment and low levels of political cynicism.[31] Both Jerald G. Bachman and Sandra J. Kenyon found weak but positive relationships between feelings of personal efficacy and low levels of political cynicism.[32] On the other hand, Jack Dennis, Harrell R. Rodgers, Jr., and George Taylor, and Samuel Long found inconsistent results that are reported below.[33]

Assumption B.4. Black children are deprived of opportunity and denied respect.

Few would deny that blacks are socially deprived. Peter M. Blau and Otis Dudley Duncan's definitive analysis of the American occupational structure clearly documented that blacks lack social opportunity.[34] Although blacks have made some progress in the past decade,[35] they still lag far behind whites on almost any measure of social equality.[36] And, while the studies cited above document the deprivation of black adults, black children are clearly disadvantaged when their parents are deprived. But black children are also directly deprived. According to the 1970 census, 87 per cent of the white children under the age of eighteen were living with both of their parents, while the comparable figure for black children was only 57 per cent.[37] Most of the measures of educational deprivation developed by Coleman showed that blacks were deprived compared with whites, although these differences often disappeared when controls for region were introduced.[38] Black children are also deprived of respect. Regardless of their social attainment, blacks are treated by many whites as inferior.

Assumption B.5. Black children have lower levels of self-confidence than white children have and, in particular, are less likely to feel they can control their social environment.

As we have documented that blacks are socially deprived, we now have strong theoretical reasons for predicting that they will have low feelings of self-confidence. Numerous studies do document such a relationship, but others find blacks to score as high or higher on measures of self-esteem as whites do. In large part, differences between these findings result from the types of measures used.

Several independently conducted studies found black children to have problems identifying as blacks.[39] According to Thomas F. Pettigrew, "These identity problems are inextricably linked with problems of self-esteem."[40] Harold Proshansky and Peggy Newton reported "considerable evidence to support the assumption that there is a direct relationship between problems in emergence of *self* and the extent to which the child's ethnic or racial membership group is socially unacceptable and subject to conspicuous deprivation."[41] They further argue that conflict in racial self-identification "tends to nourish feelings of self-doubt and a sense of inadequacy, if not actual self-hatred."[42] Recent assertions of black pride may have modified these feelings of racial rejection. Black children, for example, used to prefer white-skinned dolls.[43] According to Jeanne Spurlock, "This situation has changed since black has become beautiful. . . . Coloring books for the young child are geared to black identity; black dolls are flooding the market."[44]

Psychiatrists have painted a particularly bleak picture of low self-confidence among blacks. Abram Kardiner and Lionel Ovesey conclude that slavery, followed by continued oppression after emancipation, contributed to low self-esteem among blacks. In their case studies, some of which were with black adolescents, low self-esteem was a common reaction to attempts to control rage.[45] William H. Grier and Price M. Cobbs advanced a similar thesis, arguing that low self-esteem among blacks was a form of cultural adaptation.[46] However, Kardiner and Ovesey and Grier and Cobbs have been criticized for generalizing about an entire race from a small number of cases.[47]

While psychiatrists must rely on a small number of cases, social psychologists can study a relatively large number of persons through questionnaires and structured interviews although, of course, their techniques also face problems of validity and reliability.[48] Here, too, the results are mixed. As Morris Rosenberg and Roberta G. Simmons documented in their careful review of twelve studies conducted before 1970, blacks often scored as high as, and sometimes higher than, whites on measures of self-esteem.[49] These studies focused on feelings of personal worthiness. Other studies of personal worthiness, not cited by Rosenberg and Simmons, also showed a mixed pattern.[50] But blacks have consistently scored lower on studies measuring the extent to which they feel they can control their environment. In their massive nationwide study, Coleman and his colleagues found fairly strong racial differences in their measure of "sense of control" over the environment. On all three questions used, black children showed a much lower sense of control than did white children.[51] After an extensive review of the research literature about feelings of internal and external control, Victor Clark Joe concluded that virtually all available studies showed blacks tended to have stronger feelings of external control than whites—that is, blacks were more likely to believe that reinforcements were not under their own personal control but, rather, were controlled by powerful others, luck, chance, or fate.[52] And Samuel Long, who also summarized findings about internal-external control, concluded, "Whereas the extant research on the relationship between race and self-esteem proved equivocal, it would seem that the relationship between race and locus of control has been more clearly delineated.

Blacks experiencing social deprivation appear to manifest greater feelings of external control."[53]

Despite the evidence cited by Joe and Long, Assumption B.5 can be questioned on two grounds. First, there is the possibility, raised by Patricia Gurin and her colleagues, that the Rotter measure may not be sensitive to the realities faced by black Americans. As they write:

> The personality measure of internal-external control developed by Rotter and his associates requires the individual to choose between two explanations for success and failure—an internal explanation asserting that what happens in life is the result of skill, ability, or effort, and an external explanation asserting that success and failure are determined by fate or chance. These may be the most pertinent bases for people whose advantaged position in the social structure limits the operation of other external determinants of success and failure.
>
> But low income groups experience many external obstacles that have nothing to do with chance.... There are class-tied obstacles to many kinds of opportunities and to resources that open up other opportunities, which may be perceived correctly by low-income persons as external but not a matter of randomness or luck. For Negroes there is also the external factor of racial discrimination which operates over and beyond the class constraints they may or may not experience. Discrimination may be perceived as operating quite the opposite of chance—systematically, predictably, and reliably.[54]

Given the social realities faced by blacks, low scores on measures of self-confidence may reflect their evaluation of the social system, not just an evaluation of their own competence. Thus it is possible that low scores on self-confidence measures may have somewhat different behavioral consequences for blacks than for whites. As Gurin and her colleagues write, "Instead of depressing motivation, focusing on external forces may be motivationally healthy if it results from assessing one's chances for success against systematic and real external obstacles rather than the exigencies of an overwhelming, unpredictable fate."[55]

Second, we may question Assumption B.5 because recent assertions of black pride and the growth of black self-awareness may have boosted feelings of self-confidence among black Americans. Admittedly, our data are not adequate to determine whether recent assertions of racial pride have eroded racial differences in self-confidence. However, increased black militancy has led to feelings of racial pride.[56] The very use of the term *black,* until a decade ago a term of abuse even among blacks, attests to this change.[57] E. Earl Baughman argues that recent assertions of racial pride may have increased black feelings of self-esteem as well.[58] Being black, Baughman maintains, may protect an individual's self-esteem, since racial discrimination allows a black to blame his failures on his social environment. The bulk of the available data, however, show that black children have lower feelings of control over their environment than white children have, although we must agree with Baughman that "we badly need longitudinal studies of self-esteem in which various measures of self-esteem are used."[59]

The preceding five assumptions lead us to predict two empirical relationships that can be tested if appropriate data are available.

Empirical Consequence B.1. In social settings where blacks have higher levels of social opportunity, they should have higher feelings of political effectiveness and political trust. Controlling for social opportunity should reduce or eliminate racial differences in political attitudes.

To test this consequence adequately, it would be necessary systematically to measure levels of opportunity among blacks and to determine whether blacks with more opportunity felt more politically efficacious and trusting than those with restricted opportunities. Although such relationships can be studied, extant socialization research seldom allows for such comparisons. We can, however, test this consequence indirectly by examining levels of political efficacy and trust among blacks from different social backgrounds.

Studies of political efficacy provide fairly consistent indirect support for Empirical Consequence B.1. Analyses by Kenneth P. Langton and M. Kent Jennings, Sandra J. Kenyon, Alden J. Stevens, Schley R. Lyons, and William E. Hulbary all found that black children from higher socioeconomic backgrounds tended to have stronger feelings of political efficacy than those with lower social backgrounds, but all these analysts found that racial differences persisted even when controls for socioeconomic background were introduced.[60] Thomas S. Grotelueschen, who studied only blacks, found a strong tendency for blacks with higher socioeconomic backgrounds to score higher on feelings of political efficacy than those with lower social backgrounds. He argues, "If, as Abramson suggests, the lack of political efficacy among Blacks is a result of social deprivation, then it would seem that relatively high political efficacy levels would appear among those who enjoy lesser deprivation in upper socioeconmic strata."[61] "The findings of this study," Grotelueschen concludes, "are, of course, consistent with this supposition and appear to add further empirical support to the Abramson point of view."[62] Among studies of political efficacy that introduced controls for socioeconomic background, only Rodgers' study of North Carolina schoolchildren found no relationship between socioeconomic background and feelings of efficacy among blacks.[63]

Studies of political trust, however, do not provide consistent support for Empirical Consequence B.1. Analyses by Edward S. Greenberg, Schley R. Lyons, Anthony M. Orum and Roberta S. Cohen, and Bruce A. Campbell do show that blacks from higher socioeconomic backgrounds are more politically trusting than those from lower backgrounds but, once again, controls for socioeconomic background did not eliminate racial differences in levels of political trust.[64] However, neither Grotelueschen nor Rodgers found a relationship between social background and political trust among blacks.[65]

All the above findings provide at best an indirect test of Empirical Consequence B.1, for level of socioeconomic position only indirectly measures social opportunities.

In a sense, James W. Clarke's study of family structure and political attitudes among black children poses a more direct test of the consequence.[66] During the summer of 1969, Clarke surveyed 94 black children between the ages of five and seventeen in a lower-class neighborhood in Washington, D.C. Thirty-one of these children reported that their fathers lived at home and 63 reported that their fathers lived at home only sometimes or not at all. Clarke then applied the five-item political cynicism scale developed by M. Kent Jennings and Richard G. Niemi.[67] Among children whose father lived at home, 29 per cent scored low on political cynicism, while among those whose fathers were absent, only 5 per cent scored low. These relationships held among both younger and older children and among both boys and girls.[68] Clarke was not clear as to whether his measure of father absence was an indicator of social deprivation, or whether it revealed something about the political effects of the structure of the black family. Perhaps he concluded, both factors were at work: "It is perhaps definitional to suggest that fatherless children are the most severely victimized by the hardships of the ghetto and that the absence of fathers is only another symptom, along with the children's attitudes, of such intolerable conditions. If this is the case, father absence is not a 'determinant' but just another result of these conditions. Albeit a result that in turn undoubtedly generates negative effects of its own."[69]

Empirical Consequence B.2. Black children with high feelings of self-confidence should feel more politically efficacious and more trusting than those with low feelings of self-confidence. Controlling for feelings of self-confidence should reduce or eliminate racial differences in political attitudes.

There is some direct support for this consequence. Jack Dennis found that blacks with high self-esteem scored higher on both feelings of political effectiveness and political trust than those with low self-esteem.[70] Harrell R. Rodgers, Jr., and George Taylor found that black schoolchildren scoring high on personal efficacy were more likely to trust political leaders than those who scored low.[71] In Samuel Long's first two studies, blacks who felt they could control their environment were less likely to feel politically alienated than those who felt a lack of control. In his 1972 survey, there was a significant relationship between feelings of internal control and feelings of political efficacy, and a predicted, but not significant, relationship between feelings of internal control and political trust.[72] In his 1973 survey, Long found a strong relationship between feelings of internal control and a combined measure of political alienation. Blacks with strong feelings of internal control scored markedly lower on political alienation.[73] In none of the above studies, however, did the authors introduce controls for self-confidence to attempt to eliminate racial differences in feelings of political efficacy and trust.[74] Moreover, some data fail to support Empirical Consequence B.2. In his 1974 survey, Long found mixed results. Among blacks, low feelings of internal control were consistently and significantly correlated with feelings of political incapability, cynicism, and discontentment, but feelings of self-esteem and self-evaluation were not consistently related to these attitudes.[75] And, in his North Carolina survey, Rodgers found only negligible relationships between feelings of personal efficacy and feelings of political efficacy and cynicism.[76]

Finally, we may mention Schley R. Lyons' study, which indirectly supports Empirical Consequence B.2. Lyons predicted that a child's success in "mastering the school environment" would serve as a good predictor of feelings of political effectiveness. At every grade level, school achievement was a good predictor of feelings of political efficacy, and it was especially strongly related to feelings of political efficacy among inner-city schoolchildren.[77] Lyons argued that success in school might be a measure of self-confidence: "Achievement in school is equated with more than just intellectual ability; it is probably a manifestation of the personality as a whole. . . . ['Bright' children] tend to be self-confident, self-assured, and are free from unsubstantiated fears and apprehensions. It is quite plausible, therefore, that achievement in school measures a range of psychological predispositions that carry over into the child's attitudes about politics."[78] There was a strong relationship between school success and feelings of political efficacy among inner-city children, Lyons reasoned, because "being Negro and a low achiever significantly depresses a sense of political efficacy." "In contrast," he wrote, "high achievement, and the range of psychological predispositions that are probably measured by achievement apparently aid the Negro child in developing a sense of political effectiveness."[79] But one cannot determine from Lyons' tables whether controlling for school achievement reduces racial differences on feelings of political efficacy.[80] Moreover, Empirical Consequence B.2 also predicts that high feelings of self-confidence will contribute to high levels of political trust among black schoolchildren and, as Lyons reports, school achievement was not a good predictor of political cynicism.[81]

Lyons is among the few political socialization researchers who at least attempted to develop and to test an explanation for racial differences. His argument is theoretically interesting, but his analysis provides at best a weak test of the relationship between self-confidence and political attitudes, for school achievement is not a measure of psychological attributes. Interestingly, while Rodgers also uses school achievement as a psychological measure, he considers it to be an indirect measure of intelligence.[82]

DISCUSSIONS OF THE SOCIAL-DEPRIVATION EXPLANATION

In his authoritative review of the political-socialization literature in *Political Attitudes Through the Life Cycle,* David O. Sears discusses both the social-deprivation and the political-reality explanations.[83] Sears begins by critiquing research on "attachment to the system." Sears notes that there is considerable evidence documenting black political disaffection, but speculates that this disaffection may be aimed at the "authorities" rather than at the "regime." In other words, Sears argues that black children may be more critical of the specific authorities responsible for making and implementing political decisions, but may still support the American political system. Sears acknowledges, however, that it is difficult to differentiate empirically among these different objects of support. He correctly concludes that measures of system support, such as political trust, inherently tap support for both the authorities and the regime. But, regardless of the meaning of racial differences, Sears attempts to explain why black children tend to feel less politically powerful and trusting than white children do. He turns first to social-psychological theories.

One such approach argues that children feel vulnerable to persons with power, and therefore protect themselves by viewing authority figures as benevolent. Black children might feel more vulnerable than white children, but they do not view political authorities as more benevolent than white children do. Sears considers the social-deprivation explanation within the context of the vulnerability thesis. He writes that Abramson, in his "effort to test the ramifications of this [vulnerability] hypothesis, finds that low political trust (and low sense of political efficacy) is somewhat more common among blacks than whites, and so is low self-esteem, and in both racial groups low trust and efficacy are associated with feelings of low self-esteem." "But," Sears adds, "whether the former is due to the latter, as required by the vulnerability hypothesis, remains an unknown, since no one has yet determined that racial differences in political trust (or efficacy) disappear with self-esteem controlled, as they should." In fact, no one has even determined that racial differences in feelings of political efficacy and trust decline when controls for self-confidence are introduced. Sears, as we will see, is much more supportive of the political-reality explanation.

In his analysis of black political life, Milton D. Morris also evaluates both the social-deprivation and political-reality explanations.[84] Morris devotes a chapter to black political attitudes, and specifically discusses the attitudes of black children. As he notes, most studies of black adults and children show blacks to be politically more cynical and to feel politically less efficacious than whites do. Morris warns us to be cautious about these findings, because they rely upon questionnaires and because children may respond even if they have no real attitudes. "Nevertheless," he concludes, "the consistency of the findings and the absence of significant conflicting evidence make them convincing."[85] Morris asks why there are racial differences in political attitudes, and discusses three explanations at length; the social-deprivation explanation, the political-reality explanation, and a "sub-cultural" explanation developed by Anthony M. Orum and Roberta S. Cohen.

Morris does a fair and careful job summarizing these explanations. He directly quotes my basic summary of the social-deprivation explanation. He notes correctly that I do not test the explanation with data of my own, and further notes that "although each of the closely related propositions upon which it rests has been supported by fairly extensive research, there is room for doubt about whether the relationships postulated exist in fact."[86] At this point, Morris cites Harrell R. Rodgers, Jr.'s direct test of the social-deprivation explanation which, as we shall see, provides virtually no support for it. We have already seen that the assumptions of the explanation were not always supported by available data. However, the bulk of the available data does support the basic assumptions of the social-deprivation explanation, and there was some support for both of its empirical consequences.

Morris argues that the social deprivation of blacks is obvious. "What this [the social-deprivation] theory does," he writes, "is to suggest why the poor—or those in the society who are socially deprived—exhibit low levels of trust and efficacy." But, he adds, "It does not appear to explain black-white differences where they exist in spite of socio-economic status."[87] This is certainly correct and, although we have few firm findings, it would appear that racial differences in feelings of political efficacy and trust persist even after controls for levels of social deprivation are applied. But even if controls for social deprivation do not eliminate racial differences, the social-deprivation explanation would provide a valid partial explanation if such differences were merely reduced. As we will see, Morris, like Sears, finds the political-reality explanation more persuasive than the social-deprivation explanation.

TESTS OF THE SOCIAL-DEPRIVATION EXPLANATION

Harrell R. Rodgers, Jr., performs an extensive and imaginative test of the social-deprivation explanation with his North Carolina data.[88] He used a social-class index based upon parental education and occupation, and a three-item index that tapped the student's feelings of personal efficacy. Rodgers' measure of social position only indirectly measured social deprivation, but his personal-efficacy measure directly tapped the student's feeling that he could control his life chances.[89] Rodgers found very little support for the social-deprivation explanation. There was moderate support for Assumption B.1, for there was a slight predicted relationship between social position and feelings of personal efficacy. But neither Assumption B.2 nor B.3 were supported, for feelings of personal efficacy were not significantly related to either feelings of political efficacy or political cynicism.[90] Blacks were socially deprived compared with whites (supporting Assumption B.4), but no racial comparisons were provided to test Assumption B.5. However, all five assumptions must be supported for the explanation to be valid. In fact, Rodgers' data do not even support a "simplified" social-deprivation explanation that removes self-confidence as an intervening social-psychological variable,[91] for social position did not relate significantly to either political efficacy or to cynicism.[92]

But, not content with his simple test, Rodgers attempted to search for a more complex pattern of relationships. Personal trust, he argued, might serve as an intervening variable, for "Abramson suggests that possibly personal trust needs to be added to these relationships as an integral part of the development of personal efficacy."[93] In fact, although the social-deprivation explanation began with Erikson's discussion of trust, personal trust was not included in the basic assumptions of the social-deprivation explanation. Erikson refers to basic trust necessary to function in human society. The social-deprivation explanation incorporates M. Brewster Smith's formulation that, once a minimal level of trust is established, hope becomes the more crucial variable in explaining feelings of self-confidence. Nonetheless, Rodgers examined both direct and indirect paths through which personal trust might strengthen the social-deprivation explanation. Social deprivation, however, could not play a major role in his tests, for there was virtually no relationship between social position and feelings of personal trust.[94]

In the course of his analysis, Rodgers found two interesting relationships. There was a significant positive correlation between personal trust and feelings of political effectiveness, and a significant negative correlation between personal trust and political cynicism. In other words, blacks who had strong feelings of interpersonal trust were more likely to feel politically efficacious and were more likely to trust political leaders than were blacks who distrusted their fellow men.[95] "These findings," Rodgers wrote, "reveal that the political efficacy and political cynicism of the black students reflect in part their trust in mankind."[96]

Rodgers concluded that his data did not support the social-deprivation explanation.[97] Rodgers' test was fair and his conclusion sound. He argued, nonetheless, that the explanation deserved further study. He recognized that his measure of social position did not adequately measure social deprivation. Also, several of his variables contained little statistical variance. "More imaginatively drawn variables," he concluded, "might yield different results."[98]

Rodgers' test, however careful, was restricted to a single data base, and his survey was conducted in a setting that Rodgers himself regarded as atypical. Samuel Long, on the other hand, tested the social-deprivation explanation with three separate data sets, based upon surveys conducted in 1972, 1973, and 1974.[99] The data from Long's first two tests provided considerable support for the explanation; the data from the third test did not support it. However, in all three cases Long concluded that his data did not support the social-deprivation explanation, for in each case he advanced hypotheses that do not follow from the explanation and then failed to support these hypotheses. I will begin by reporting Long's findings and will then turn to his interpretation of them.

Long's 1972 survey measured feelings of political incapability and discontentment.[100] His first scale clearly measured feelings of political effectiveness (or ineffectiveness), and he considered his second scale a measure of political distrust.[101] Although he did not directly measure social deprivation, he did provide a theoretically sound measure of self-confidence that taps the respondent's feelings that he can control his environment.[102] Long found support for Assumption B.2, B.3, and B.5. Children with strong feelings of personal effectiveness were more likely to have strong feelings of political effectiveness; they were also more likely to score high on political trust. In addition, black children had weaker feelings of personal effectiveness than white children had.[103] Long also found support for Empirical Consequence B.2. Black children with strong feelings of internal control were more likely to feel politically efficacious than those with low feelings of self-confidence. Blacks with strong feelings of internal control also scored higher on political trust, although this relationship was not statistically significant.[104] Long could have provided a stronger test, however, by attempting to eliminate or to reduce racial differences in feelings of political efficacy and trust by controlling for self-confidence, but no such controls were introduced.

Long's 1973 survey also used his measure of political incapability and discontentment, but he combined these scales to form an overall measure of political alienation.[105] Combining these scales weakened Long's test, for although feelings of efficacy and trust are usually interrelated, political alienation is best conceptualized as multidimensional.[106] Moreover, the correlates of political efficacy and of political trust are not always identical and, in our review of the socialization literature (including Long's first test), we found that feelings of self-confidence more consistently correlated with feelings of political efficacy than they did with feelings of political trust.[107] As with his first test, Long did not directly measure levels of social deprivation, but he did build a scale that measured feelings of internal control.[108]

Long found a substantial relationship between feelings of internal control and feelings of political alienation. Since his measures of political incapability and discontent were highly interrelated, this finding can be considered support for Assumption B.2 and B.3.[109] Long also found that black children had weaker feelings of internal control than white children had, thus supporting Assumption B.5.[110] Lastly, Long found support for Empirical Consequence B.2, for among blacks there was a very strong relationship between feelings of internal control and low levels of political alienation.[111] In other words, blacks who felt they could control their environment were much less likely to feel politically alienated than those who felt personally ineffacious. Once again, Long's test would have been stronger if he had attempted to eliminate or reduce racial differences in political alienation by controlling for feelings of self-confidence.

In his 1974 survey,[112] Long measured feelings of political incapability and discontentment but also added a more conventional measure of political cynicism, as well as a measure of political estrangement which, in our view, taps neither feelings of political efficacy nor of trust.[113] Long's result was strikingly different from his first two tests, for with his St. Louis data he found blacks to feel marginally more efficacious and trusting than whites.[114] His test of the social-deprivation explanation was based upon both measures of self-esteem and of locus of control.[115] Whereas the self-esteem measures were not consistently related to feelings of political efficacy and trust, the locus of control measures provided support for Assumptions B.2 and B.3. Students who felt they could control their environment were consistently more likely to feel politically efficacious and trusting.[116] Moreover, these relations obtained among blacks, providing support for Empirical Consequence B.2. However, the St. Louis data do not support the social-deprivation explanation, for Assumption B.5 was not supported. Black children scored somewhat higher on self-esteem than whites, and there were no racial differences in feelings of locus of control.[117]

In addition to examining the relationship of each personality measure to each measure of political alienation, Long also tested the social-deprivation explanation in these two ways: by combining his personality measures to form an overall measure of self-confidence, and by combining his efficacy, trust, and estrangement measures to form a political alienation scale. This test showed that among whites feelings of self-confidence were negatively related to political alienation, whereas among blacks those with high feelings of self-confidence were somewhat more alienated than those with lower feelings of self-confidence.[118] But a test using combined measures is weaker than a test using each measure separately. As we have already argued, Long's 1973 test was weakened by using a combined measure of efficacy and trust. The 1974 test was further weakened by using an aggregate measure of self-confidence, for, as Fred I. Greenstein points out, research suggests that it is important to disaggregate global personality traits.[119] Long's own data clearly suggest that Greenstein was correct, for he derived markedly different results with his measures of locus of control than with his measures of self-esteem, and by combining these measures he conceals these differences.

In all three tests Long concluded that there was little support for the social-deprivation explanation. But with each test Long advanced hypotheses that do not follow from the explanation. Lacking actual measures of social deprivation, Long used a measure of "perceived social deprivation," based upon children's responses to a self-anchoring scale.[120] Perceived social deprivation was not systematically related to feelings of self-confidence and did not relate to feelings of political effectiveness and trust. But the social-deprivation explanation postulates the effects of actual deprivation upon feelings of self-confidence, not the effects of perceptions of deprivation. Long's measure of perceived social deprivation might be useful in testing the "simplified" social-deprivation explanation to be developed below. If persons who are deprived are to blame political authorities, one might argue, they must recognize that they are deprived. Long's research suggests that adolescents who feel socially deprived do not blame political authorities for their condition. But it does not provide a test of the social-deprivation explanation as it was formulated.

Long also consistently argued that the relationship between psychological variables and political attitudes should be stronger among blacks than among whites. But this does not follow from the social-deprivation explanation. While Empirical Consequences B.1 and B.2 specifically focus on expected relationships among blacks, the social-psychological correlates of political efficacy and trust should be similar for both races.

Last, we may briefly mention Bruce A. Campbell's attempt to test the explanation.[121] In his study of Atlanta high school seniors, conducted between November 1973 and March 1974, he found that blacks were much more likely than whites to have anti-administration views of Watergate.[122] Whereas 74 per cent of the black students had an anti-administration view, only 42 per cent of the whites did. Campbell speculated that social deprivation might account for these racial differences, and he advanced two hypotheses. First, there may be a simple relationship between social deprivation and attitudes toward Watergate that might explain racial differences. Second, this relationship might be explained by the intervening variable of personal efficacy.

The data supported neither hypothesis. Blacks were deprived compared with whites (with father's occupational level used as a measure of deprivation), but social deprivation was not related to attitudes to Watergate for either blacks or for whites. Moreover, perceived occupational deprivation was not significantly related to attitudes toward Watergate for either race. Since the first hypothesis was not supported, the second hypothesis, which postulated the role of an intervening variable, was also rejected. In fact, feelings of personal efficacy were weakly related to both social deprivation and to attitudes toward Watergate. "On the basis of the sum of this evidence," Campbell concluded, "we reject the social deprivation hypothesis."[123]

It is questionable, however, whether Campbell's evidence is appropriate for testing the social-deprivation explanation. The explanation attempts to account for racial differences in more generalized feelings of political efficacy and trust, not evaluations of a specific political event. Not surprisingly, attitudes toward Watergate, at least at the early stages of the revelations, were affected mainly by partisanship.[124] Moreover, there is some evidence that attitudes toward Watergate were only weakly related to more generalized feelings of political trust.[125] At best, Campbell's test of the social-deprivation explanation is weak, for he relied upon a dependent variable that had questionable validity. However, based upon information provided to

me directly by Campbell, I suspect he would have found little support
for the explanation even if he had focused on his more appropriate
measure of political trust.[126]

EVALUATION OF THE
SOCIAL-DEPRIVATION EXPLANATION

The social-deprivation explanation is a plausible partial explanation for racial differences in feelings of political efficacy and political
trust. We have sound theoretical and some empirical support for each
of the five basic assumptions of the social-deprivation explanation, and
some empirical support for both empirical consequences (although
support for Empirical Consequence B.1 was indirect). The bulk of the
available evidence supports each of its five assumptions, although Assumptions B.2, B.3, and B.5 were not always supported by available
data. Moreover, three of the five attempts to test the explanation found
little support for it. Rodgers found almost no support for the causal
relationships suggested by the explanation, and, while Long found
some support with his first two surveys, his St. Louis data did not
support it. Last, while Campbell's test relied upon attitudes toward
Watergate, we suspect that he would have found little support using
his more generalized measure of political trust.

The social-deprivation explanation has several major problems.
First, it is complicated, for it depends upon five assumptions. Second, it
relies upon an intervening social-psychological variable—feelings of
self-confidence. The research literature of self-confidence has been
marked by conceptual confusion and by mixed empirical results. The
explanation could be simplified greatly, and the conceptual problems of
the self-confidence literature ignored, if this intervening variable were
dropped.

Perhaps persons who are socially deprived resent the political authorities who are responsible for the authoritative allocation of societal
values. Since they receive few rewards, they may conclude they are
politically powerless, and their resentment may lead them to conclude
that political leaders cannot be trusted. In a modern industrial state
the government is assumed to be responsible for the welfare of the
citizenry and the relatively disadvantaged can blame their misfor-
tunes, at least in part, on governmental authorities. And the disadvantaged may need no complex reasoning to blame political authorities,
for their feelings of political powerlessness and cynicism may spring
from a more generalized resentment against all authorities. Even children might resent these authorities, either because they learn these
attitudes from adults or from peers, or because these attitudes are a
generalized manifestation of system blame.

If we were to eliminate feelings of self-confidence as an intervening social-psychological variable, Assumptions B.1, B.2, B.3, and B.5 could be dropped, and Assumption B.4 would remain. But two new assumptions would have to precede it:

New Assumption B.1. Persons who are socially deprived tend to conclude they are politically powerless.

New Assumption B.2. Persons who are socially deprived tend to resent political authorities and conclude they cannot be trusted.

Assumption B.4 would become New Assumption B.3.

While this modified formulation has the virtue of simplicity, it has two fundamental problems. First, it leaves open the question of whether persons who are socially deprived must feel they are deprived, whereas the original formulation avoided the concept of relative deprivation. To support this explanation must the researcher demonstrate the presence of absolute deprivation, feelings of relative deprivation, or both? Second, and more important, we must explain why deprived *children* come to blame political authorities. Political authorities, after all, are relatively removed from most acts that deprive black preadults. A black child who sees no prospect of future employment may blame his school, or employers, or the "system," but should we expect him to blame *political* authorities? A black child who feels he is getting a bad education may blame his teachers, but can we expect a schoolchild to conclude that his inferior education results from his lack of power to influence political authorities or from the dishonesty of public officials? Moreover, the "simplified" social-deprivation explanation is scarcely distinct from the political-reality explanation that we will advance as a fourth possible cause of racial differences in political attitudes.

Both the social-deprivation explanation, as formulated, and the "simplified" version share another fundamental problem. Neither can be used to explain the time-series pattern that we discovered when examining political trust. Blacks were socially deprived before the summer of 1967; why, then, were they as trusting as whites? In fact, after 1965, the relative income of blacks, compared with that of whites, began to improve.[127] Presumably, social deprivation did not increase markedly during and after the summer of 1967. Perceptions about deprivation may have changed, but they did not result from increased economic and social deprivation.[128]

NOTES

1. Erik H. Erikson, *Childhood and Society,* 2d ed. (New York: Norton, 1963), p. 249.

2. *Ibid.,* p. 250.

3. M. Brewster Smith, *Social Psychology and Human Values* (Chicago: Aldine, 1969), p. 219.

4. *Ibid.*

5. *Ibid.*

6. *Ibid.,* p. 247.

7. For an extensive review of these findings, see Victor Clark Joe, "Review of the Internal-External Control Construct as a Personality Variable," *Psychological Reports,* 28 (1971), pp. 619–640.

8. James S. Coleman et al., *Equality of Educational Opportunity* (Washington, D.C.: U.S. Government Printing Office, 1966), p. 288. Coleman relied on the following three questions:

"(1) Agree or disagree: Good luck is more important than hard work for success . . .

"(2) Agree or disagree: Every time I try to get ahead, something or somebody stops me . . .

"(3) People like me don't have much of a chance to be successful in life."

9. *Ibid.,* pp. 288–290; pp. 324–325.

10. *Ibid.,* p. 321.

11. For an interesting theoretical argument to support this thesis, see Warren G. Haggstrom, "The Power of the Poor," in *Mental Health of the Poor: New Treatment Approaches for Low Income People,* eds. Frank Riessman, Jerome Cohen, and Arthur Pearl (New York: Free Press, 1964), pp. 205–223. See also Alex Inkeles, "Social Structure and the Socialization of Competence," *Harvard Educational Review,* 36 (Summer 1966), pp. 265–283.

12. Robert E. Lane, *Political Life: Why and How People Get Involved in Politics* (Glencoe, Ill.: Free Press, 1959), p. 149.

13. Angus Campbell, Philip E. Converse, Warren E. Miller, and Donald E. Stokes, *The American Voter* (New York: Wiley, 1960), pp. 516–519.

14. *Ibid.*

15. Paul M. Sniderman, *Personality and Democratic Politics* (Berkeley: University of California Press, 1975). See pp. 24–63 for a discussion of these dimensions, and p. 53 for the specific items used to build these measures of self-esteem.

16. *Ibid.,* pp. 80–81.

17. *Ibid.,* p. 82.

18. Roberta S. Sigel, "Bases of Political and Civic Involvement among Rural High School Students—Internal/External Control and Involvement," revised version of paper presented at 67th Annual Meeting of American Political Science Association, Chicago, September 1971, p. 20. See also Sigel, "Psychological Antecedents and Political Involvement: The Utility of the Concept of Locus-of-Control," *Social Science Quarterly,* 56 (September 1975), pp. 315–323.

Sigel used Julian B. Rotter's measure of internal-external control. See Rotter, "Generalized Expectancies for Internal versus External Control of Reinforcements," *Psychological Monographs: General and Applied,* 80 (Whole No.

609), 1966; and Rotter, "Generalized Expectancies for Interpersonal Trust," *American Psychologist,* 26 (May 1971), pp. 443–452. In Rotter's terminology, persons who feel they can control their environment are labeled "internals." Those who believe that rewards and punishments are not related to their own efforts are "externals."

19. See Sandra J. Kenyon, "The Development of Political Cynicism: A Study of Political Socialization," unpublished Ph.D. dissertation, Massachusetts Institute of Technology, 1970, p. 82; Jack Dennis, *Political Learning in Childhood and Adolescence: A Study of Fifth, Eighth, and Eleventh Graders in Milwaukee, Wisconsin* (Madison: Wisconsin Research and Development Center for Cognitive Learning, 1969), p. 83; Samuel Long, "Malevolent Estrangement: Political Alienation and Political [Violence] Justification Among Black and White Adolescents," *Youth and Society,* 7 (December 1975), pp. 99–129, at p. 109; and Long, "Cognitive-Perceptual Factors in the Political Alienation Process: A Test of Six Models," paper presented at 34th Annual Meeting of Midwest Political Science Association, Chicago, April-May 1976, pp. 16–17.

Harrell R. Rodgers, Jr., however, reported a very weak positive relationship between feelings of personal efficacy and feelings of political efficacy. See Rodgers, "Toward Explanation of the Political Efficacy and Political Cynicism of Black Adolescents: An Exploratory Study," *American Journal of Political Science,* 18 (May 1974), pp. 257–282, at pp. 268–269.

20. See Herbert L. Mirels, "Dimensions of Internal Versus External Control," *Journal of Consulting and Clinical Psychology,* 34 (April 1970), pp. 226–228. However, Mirels focused on the respondent's assessment of the effect citizens could have in influencing political institutions, not the extent to which the respondent thought he or she could influence those institutions.

21. William F. Stone, *The Psychology of Politics* (New York: Free Press, 1974), p. 196.

22. *Ibid.,* p. 197.

23. Lane, *Political Life,* p. 164.

24. Sniderman, *Personality and Democratic Politics,* pp. 165–222.

25. *Ibid.,* p. 188.

26. *Ibid.*

27. *Ibid.,* pp. 192–193.

28. *Ibid.*

29. Stanley Allen Renshon, *Psychological Needs and Political Behavior: A Theory of Personality and Political Efficacy* (New York: Free Press, 1974).

30. *Ibid.,* p. 156.

31. Sigel, "Bases of Political and Civic Involvement," p. 20; and Sigel, "Psychological Antecedents and Political Involvement."

32. Jerald G. Bachman, *Youth in Transition, Volume 2: The Impact of Family Background and Intelligence on Tenth Grade Boys* (Ann Arbor, Mich.: Institute for Social Research, 1970), p. 242; Kenyon, "The Development of Political Cynicism: A Study of Political Socialization," p. 77, as well as Sandra Kenyon Schwartz, "Patterns of Cynicism: Differential Political Socialization

among Adolescents," in *New Direction in Political Socialization,* eds. David C. Schwartz and Sandra Kenyon Schwartz (New York: Free Press, 1975), pp. 188–202, at p. 194.

33. See pp. 45–46.

34. Peter M. Blau and Otis Dudley Duncan, *The American Occupational Structure* (New York: Wiley, 1967), pp. 207–227. See also Paul M. Siegel, "On the Cost of Being a Negro," *Sociological Inquiry,* 35 (Winter 1965), pp. 41–57.

35. See, for example, Ben J. Wattenberg and Richard M. Scammon, "Black Progress and Liberal Rhetoric," *Commentary,* 55 (April 1973), pp. 35–44, for a somewhat overoptimistic assessment of black social and economic progress.

36. For the most compelling recent evidence documenting the economic and social deprivation of black Americans, see Sar A. Levitan, William B. Johnston, and Robert Taggart, *Still a Dream: The Changing Status of Blacks Since 1960* (Cambridge, Mass.: Harvard University Press, 1975).

37. U.S. Bureau of the Census, *1970 Census of Population: General Social and Economic Characteristics* (Washington, D.C.: U.S. Government Printing Office, 1972), Table 89.

38. Coleman et al., *Equality,* pp. 35–212. U.S. Commission on Civil Rights, *Racial Isolation in the Public Schools, Volume 1* (Washington, D.C.: U.S. Government Printing Office, 1967), pp. 96–100. For a more recent interpretation of the Coleman data that emphasizes the similarity between black and white schools, see Christopher S. Jencks, "The Coleman Report and Conventional Wisdom," in *On Equality of Educational Opportunity,* eds. Frederick Mosteller and Daniel P. Moynihan (New York: Vintage Books, 1972), pp. 69–115.

39. See Thomas F. Pettigrew, *A Profile of the American Negro* (Princeton, N.J.: Van Nostrand, 1964), pp. 27–55; and Harold Proshansky and Peggy Newton, "The Nature and Meaning of Negro Self-Identity," in *Social Class, Race, and Psychological Development,* eds. Martin Deutsch, Irwin Katz, and Arthur R. Jensen (New York: Holt, Rinehart, and Winston, 1968), pp. 178–218.

40. Pettigrew, *A Profile,* p. 9.

41. Proshansky and Newton, "Nature and Meaning," p. 182.

42. *Ibid.,* p. 191.

43. The classic study was conducted in the late 1930s by Kenneth B. Clark and Mamie K. Clark, "The Development of 'Consciousness of Self and the Emergence of Racial Identification in Negro Preschool Children," *Journal of Social Psychology,* 10 (November 1939), pp. 591–599.

44. Jeanne Spurlock, "Problems of Identification in Young Black Children—Static or Changing," *Journal of the National Medical Association,* 61 (November 1969), pp. 504–507, 532, at p. 506.

45. Abram Kardiner and Lionel Ovesey, *The Mark of Oppression: Explorations in the Personality of the American Negro* (Cleveland: World, 1951).

46. William H. Grier and Price M. Cobbs, *Black Rage* (New York: Basic Books, 1968).

47. For a criticism of both sets of authors, see Alexander Thomas and

Samuel Sillen, *Racism and Psychiatry* (Secausus, N.J.: Citadel Press, 1972), pp. 45–56. Thomas and Sillen also cite other critics of these authors.

48. Just as psychoanalysts have been criticized for studying too few cases, social psychologists have been criticized for using crude measures that rely upon paper-and-pencil questionnaires. However, social psychologists have usually been more careful in validating their measures than political scientists have been in validating measures of political attitudes.

49. Morris Rosenberg and Roberta G. Simmons, *Black and White Self-Esteem: The Urban School Child* (Washington, D.C.: American Sociological Association, Arnold and Caroline Rose Monograph Series in Sociology, 1971), pp. 5–8. The Rosenberg-Simmons study of Baltimore children, conducted in the spring of 1968, showed black children to score higher on self-esteem than white children did.

Rosenberg's measure of self-esteem, which has been widely used, is also discussed in Rosenberg's *Society and the Adolescent Self-Image* (Princeton, N.J.: Princeton University Press, 1965). His earlier study, conducted in high schools in New York State, found blacks to have lower self-esteem than whites, although differences were small (see pp. 303–304).

50. For example, John D. McCarthy and William L. Yancey challenge the view that blacks have lower self-esteem than whites, arguing that when social class is controlled blacks should have similar levels of self-esteem. (See "Uncle Tom and Mr. Charlie: Metaphysical Pathos in the Study of Racism and Personal Disorganization," *American Journal of Sociology,* 76 [January 1971], pp. 648–672.) In another article, Yancey, along with Leo Rigsby and John McCarthy, presents mixed results, but argues that multivariate analyses demonstrate that race has little independent effect on levels of self-esteem. (See "Social Position and Self-Evaluation: The Relative Importance of Race," *American Journal of Sociology,* 78 [September 1972], pp. 338–359.) However, in a fascinating study of a small number of three-, four-, and five-year-olds, Judith D.R. Porter found blacks to have much lower levels of self-esteem than whites. (See *Black Child, White Child: The Development of Racial Attitudes* [Cambridge, Mass.: Harvard University Press, 1971], pp. 141–161.)

51. Coleman et al., *Equality,* pp. 320–321.

52. Joe, "Review of the Internal-External Control Construct," pp. 623–625.

53. Long, "Malevolent Estrangement," p. 105.

54. Patricia Gurin, Gerald Gurin, Rosina C. Lao, and Muriel Beattie, "Internal-External Control in the Motivational Dynamics of Negro Youth," *Journal of Social Issues,* 25 (Summer 1969), pp. 29–53, at pp. 32–33.

55. *Ibid.,* p. 33. See also John R. Forward and Jay R. Williams, "Internal-External Control and Black Militancy," *Journal of Social Issues,* 26 (Winter 1970), pp. 75–92.

56. See, for example, Gloria J. Powell and Marielle Fuller, "School Desegregation and Self-Concept," paper presented at 47th Annual Meeting of American Orthopsychiatric Association, San Francisco, March 1970; Edward S. Greenberg, "Black Children, Self-Esteem and the Liberation Movement,"

Politics and Society, 2 (Spring 1972), pp. 293–307; and David O. Sears and John B. McConahay, *The Politics of Violence: The New Urban Blacks and the Watts Riot* (Boston: Houghton Mifflin, 1973), p. 188.

57. See Charles E. Billings, "Black Activists and the Schools," *The High School Journal,* 54 (November 1970), pp. 96–107; and Nathan Caplan, "The New Ghetto Man: A Review of Recent Empirical Studies," *Journal of Social Issues,* 26 (Winter 1970), pp. 59–73, at pp. 66–67.

58. E. Earl Baughman, *Black Americans: A Psychological Analysis* (New York: Academic Press, 1971), p. 46. Rosenberg and Simmons, however, argue that there are no adequate data to test the thesis that black self-esteem has risen as a result of increased black militancy. See *Black and White Self-Esteem,* p. 8.

59. Baughman, *Black Americans,* p. 53.

60. See Kenneth P. Langton and M. Kent Jennings, "Political Socialization and the High School Civics Curriculum in the United States," *American Political Science Review,* 62 (September 1968), pp. 852–867, at p. 861; Sandra J. Kenyon, "The Development of Political Cynicism among Negro and White Adolescents," paper presented at 65th Annual Meeting of American Political Science Association, New York, September 1969, p. 18; Schley R. Lyons, "The Political Socialization of Ghetto Children: Efficacy and Cynicism," *Journal of Politics,* 32 (May 1970), pp. 288–304, at pp. 295–296; Alden J. Stevens, "Children's Acquisition of Regime Norms in Subcultures of Race and Class: The Problem of System Maintenance," unpublished Ph.D. dissertation, University of Maryland, 1969, pp. 66–69; and William E. Hulbary, "Adolescent Political Self-Images and Political Involvement: The Relative Effects of High School Black Studies Courses and Prior Political Socialization," unpublished Ph.D. dissertation, University of Iowa, 1972, pp. 50–64.

61. Thomas S. Grotelueschen, "The Political Orientations of Black Children in Northern Florida," unpublished Ph.D. dissertation, University of Wisconsin, 1973, pp. 83–84. Grotelueschen was discussing the social-deprivation explanation as it was developed in my paper, "Political Efficacy and Political Trust among Black Schoolchildren: Four Explanations," revised version of paper presented at Conference on Political Theory and Political Education, Michigan State University. (Revised paper dated May 1971.)

62. Grotelueschen, "The Political Orientations of Black Children," p. 84.

63. Rodgers, "Toward Explanation," p. 268.

64. Edward S. Greenberg, "Political Socialization to Support of the System: A Comparison of Black and White Children," unpublished Ph.D. dissertation, University of Wisconsin, 1969, pp. 295–296; Lyons, "The Political Socialization of Ghetto Children," pp. 295–296; and Anthony M. Orum and Roberta S. Cohen, "The Development of Political Orientations among Black and White Children," *American Sociological Review,* 38 (February 1973), pp. 62–74, at p. 66. Data from Campbell are based upon a personal communication. For a more detailed report of Campbell's findings, see note 126.

65. Grotelueschen, "The Political Orientations of Black Children," p. 89; Rodgers, "Toward Explanation," p. 268.

In their analysis of the 1965 Michigan SRC survey of high school seniors, M. Kent Jennings and Richard G. Niemi report that parental occupation was not related to feelings of political trust, but they did not discuss this relationship among the subset of black schoolchildren. See *The Political Character of Adolescence: The Influence of Families and Schools* (Princeton, N.J.: Princeton University Press, 1974), p. 144.

66. James W. Clarke, "Family Structure and Political Socialization among Urban Black Children," *American Journal of Political Science,* 17 (May 1973), pp. 302–315.

67. See pp. 151–152 in Appendix C for a list of these questions. Clarke reports that the item-total correlations of the five items ranged from .49 to .82 (gammas).

68. Clarke, "Family Structure and Political Socialization," pp. 310–311.

69. *Ibid.,* p. 315.

70. Dennis, *Political Learning in Childhood and Adolescence,* pp. 82–83.

71. Harrell R. Rodgers, Jr., and George Taylor, "The Policeman as an Agent of Regime Legitimation," *Midwest Journal of Political Science,* 15 (February 1971), pp. 72–86, at p. 84.

72. Long, "Malevolent Estrangement," p. 109.

73. Long, "Socialization to Revolt: Political Alienation and Political Violence Condonation among White and Black Youth," paper presented at 70th Annual Meeting of American Political Science Association, Chicago, August-September 1974, p. 19.

74. However, all these studies did examine the relationship between self-confidence and political attitudes among whites, and the results are mixed. Dennis found that, among both blacks and whites, children with high ego strength were more likely to believe that government officials would be responsive than were children with low ego strength. He found high ego strength to be positively related to political trust among black children, but not among whites. Like Dennis, Rodgers and Taylor found that high feelings of personal efficacy were related to feelings of political trust among black children, but not among whites. Long, however, found a different pattern. With his 1972 survey he found that the relationships between feelings of internal control and feelings of political efficacy and trust were higher among whites than among blacks. And with his 1973 survey he found that among children of both races those with high feelings of self-confidence were less politically alienated than those with low feelings of self-confidence.

75. Long, "Political Alienation among Black and White Adolescents: A Test of the Social Deprivation and Political Reality Models," *American Politics Quarterly,* 4 (July 1976), pp. 267–303, at pp. 280–281. Long also found a similar pattern among whites. In his May 1975 survey of 460 Evansville, Indiana, high school students, Long found that students with feelings of internal control were more likely to feel politically efficacious and trusting than those with feelings of external control. Self-esteem measures, on the other hand, were not related to political trust. However, Long did not present these relationships

among his subset of black respondents. See "Cognitive-Perceptual Factors," pp. 16–17.

76. Rodgers, "Toward Explanation," p. 269. Rodgers did not present these relationships among white children.

77. Lyons, "The Political Socialization of Ghetto Children," pp. 299–300.

78. *Ibid.*, p. 302.

79. *Ibid.*

80. In the three tables where Lyons presented the relationship between school achievement and political attitudes, he did not show differences according to race (*Ibid.*, pp. 298–300). Thus, the reader cannot determine the extent to which controlling for school achievement may have reduced racial differences.

81. *Ibid.*, p. 301.

82. Rodgers, "Toward Explanation," p. 273. See also pp. 71–72 below.

83. David O. Sears, *Political Attitudes Through the Life Cycle* (San Francisco: Freeman, forthcoming). As Sears' book is still in press, pagination cannot be provided. Quotations from Sears' book may be altered somewhat in his final version.

Sears' discussion of both the social-deprivation and the political-reality explanations is based upon my discussion in "Political Efficacy and Political Trust among Black Schoolchildren: Two Explanations," *Journal of Politics,* 34 (November 1972), pp. 1243–1275.

84. Milton D. Morris, *The Politics of Black Americans* (New York: Harper and Row, 1975), pp. 119–145. Morris' discussion of my explanations is also based upon my discussion in the November 1972 *Journal of Politics.*

85. Morris, *The Politics of Black Americans,* p. 142.

86. *Ibid.*, p. 143.

87. *Ibid.*

88. Rodgers, "Towards Explanation." All of Rodgers' tests were based upon my formulation in "Political Efficacy and Political Trust among Black Schoolchildren: Four Explanations."

89. Rodgers, "Toward Explanation," p. 268.

90. *Ibid.*, p. 269.

91. See pp. 54–55.

92. Rodgers, "Towards Explanation," p. 268.

93. *Ibid.*, p. 269.

94. *Ibid.*, pp. 269–270.

95. *Ibid.*, p. 270.

96. *Ibid.*

97. Rodgers conducted one additional test of the social-deprivation explanation. In my May 1971 paper I had argued that blacks in integrated schools might have more opportunity than those in segregated schools and that, as a consequence, blacks in integrated schools should feel more politically efficacious and trusting. Rodgers found that blacks in integrated schools were mar-

ginally less efficacious and trusting than those in segregated schools. ("Toward Explanation," p. 271.) I had already concluded that my argument about the effects of integrated schools was weak, and had dropped it from my *Journal of Politics* article. In her recent study, Nancy H. St. John carefully evaluates research from 40 studies of desegregation that examined self-confidence among black children. The results yielded a very mixed pattern. See *School Desegregation: Outcomes for Children* (New York: Wiley-Interscience, 1975), pp. 48–55.

98. Rodgers, "Toward Explanation," p. 271.

99. All Long's tests of the social-deprivation explanation, as well as his test of the political-reality explanation, were based upon my formulation in the November 1972 *Journal of Politics*.

100. For a discussion of Long's 1972 survey, see his "Malevolent Estrangement." For an earlier version of this article that presents Long's findings in somewhat greater detail, see his "Malevolent Estrangement: Political Alienation and Political Violence Justification among Black and White Adolescents," paper presented at 32d Annual Meeting of Midwest Political Science Association, Chicago, April, 1974. All citations to "Malevolent Estrangement," refer to the published version of his paper.

101. See Long, "Malevolent Estrangement," p. 124. Long's discontentment scale taps the extent to which respondents believe the government works for the benefit of the average citizen and whether he believes the government to be competent. It does not measure beliefs about trustworthiness of government officials. See Appendix C for items used to build Long's political discontentment scale.

102. Long employed a four-item scale that measured feelings of internal control. See his "Malevolent Estrangement," pp. 123–124.

103. *Ibid.*, p. 108.

104. Long, "Malevolent Estrangement," p. 109.

105. For a discussion of Long's 1973 survey, see his "Socialization to Revolt."

106. This is best demonstrated by Ada W. Finifter, "Dimensions of Political Alienation," *American Political Science Review,* 64 (June 1970), pp. 389–410. See also her discussion in Finifter, ed., *Alienation and the Social System* (New York: Wiley, 1972), pp. 3–11.

107. See p. 46.

108. Here Long combined one measure based upon semantic differential items and a slightly modified version of Hanna Levenson's Chance Control scale and her Powerful Others Control scale. See "Socialization to Revolt," p. 18; notes 51, 52.

109. Long, "Socialization to Revolt," p. 19.

110. Based upon a personal communication.

111. Long, "Socialization to Revolt," p. 19.

112. For a discussion of Long's 1974 survey, see his "Political Alienation." For an earlier test of the social-deprivation explanation that uses the 1974

data, see Long, "Sociopolitical Antecedents of Political Alienation among Black and White Adolescents: Social Deprivation and/or Political Reality?," paper presented at the 70th Annual Meeting of the American Sociological Association, San Francisco, August, 1975. In addition to the some 370 blacks surveyed by Long, about 50 students who were neither white nor black were grouped with blacks in his analysis.

113. Long, "Political Alienation," p. 296. The political estrangement scale is made up of the following four items:

"When I think about government and politics in the United States, I consider myself an outsider."

"I tend to identify myself with and feel closely associated with American politics and government." (Reflected so that disagreement is scored as estrangement.)

"When I hear or read about the politics and governmental system of the United States, I feel that I am part of that system." (Reflected so that disagreement is scored as estrangement.)

"When I think about the government in Washington, I don't feel as if it's my government."

114. See Appendix A for the basic results of Long's survey. Long also reports that racial differences were not significant on any of his four measures of political alienation. See "Political Alienation," pp. 278–280.

115. Long used Rosenberg's self-esteem scale as well as semantic differential items to measure self-esteem, and Levenson's Chance Control and Powerful Others Control scales to measure locus of control.

116. Long presented the relationship between two separate locus of control measures and each of his four political alienation scales for both blacks and whites. He reports that of the 16 correlations, only two failed to support the thesis that low feelings of self-confidence would correlate positively with feelings of political alienation. (See "Political Alienation," pp. 280–281.) But the two correlations that do not support this thesis were between feelings of internal control and Long's political estrangement scale, which we view as neither a measure of political efficacy nor of political trust.

117. Long, "Political Alienation," pp. 280–281.

118. Ibid., pp. 280–283.

119. See Fred I. Greenstein, "Personality and Politics," in Handbook of Political Science, Volume 2: Micropolitical Theory, eds. Fred I. Greenstein and Nelson W. Polsby (Reading, Mass.: Addison-Wesley, 1975), pp. 1–92, at p. 53.

120. Children were presented with a nine-step scale and asked to rate themselves on the appropriate rung (from the worst possible life to the best possible life) for three time periods: the present, five years in the past, and five years in the future. Perceived social deprivation was measured by the standardized sum of the adolescent's responses over three time periods. See "Malevolent Estrangement," p. 107; "Socialization to Revolt," pp. 17–18; and Long, "Political Alienation," p. 276. In Long's third test, he also used a four-item scale in which the respondents compared their families' situation with that of most families, and their own job opportunities, income opportunities,

and housing opportunities with those most people have. See "Political Alienation," p. 277.

121. See Bruce A. Campbell, "Racial Differences in the Reaction to Watergate: Some Implications for Political Support," *Youth and Society,* 7 (June 1976), pp. 439–460. Campbell's test was based upon my formulation in the November 1972 *Journal of Politics.*

122. Campbell's measure relied upon a series of open-ended questions in which students were asked whether they had heard of Watergate (all had), and asked how they evaluated the events. Campbell also employed a three-item political trust scale that tapped generalized attitudes toward trust, and we have reported his findings using this measure in Appendix A. However, his test of the explanation relied upon attitudes toward Watergate.

123. Campbell, "Racial Differences," p. 449.

124. See Campbell, "Racial Differences," pp. 444–447, and Marjorie Randon Hershey and David B. Hill, "Watergate and Preadults' Attitudes Toward the President," *American Journal of Political Science,* 19 (November 1975), pp. 703–726, at pp. 708–714.

125. See the analysis of the 1974 University of Michigan SRC-CPS post-election survey by Arthur H. Miller and his colleagues (Arthur H. Miller, Jeffrey Brudney, and Peter Joftis, "Presidential Crises and Political Support: The Impact of Watergate on Attitudes Toward Institutions," paper presented at 33rd Annual Meeting of Midwest Political Science Association, Chicago, May 1975, pp. 15–16). Campbell did not report the relationship between attitudes toward Watergate and his three-item political trust scale.

126. Campbell's personal communication to me, upon which the results in Appendix A are based, show that, among blacks, students with high socioeconomic location (based upon an additive measure) scored slightly higher on trust than those with lower socioeconomic locations ($\bar{X}$ for high SEL blacks =2.88; $\bar{X}$ for low SEL blacks=2.83).For whites this relationship was even weaker ($\bar{X}$ for high SEL whites=3.27; $\bar{X}$ for low SEL whites=3.25). So, although blacks had lower socioeconomic locations than whites, controls for socioeconomic location would do little to reduce racial differences in political trust. However, other relationships postulated by Campbell's test, such as that between perceived occupational deprivation and political trust, cannot be assessed with the data available to me.

127. For a discussion of changing income patterns during this period, see Levitan, Johnston, and Taggart, *Still a Dream,* pp. 13–43.

128. In a critique of my earlier work, Ted Tapper argues that black riots "could be seen as a delayed response to increasing relative deprivation." (See Ted Tapper, *Political Education and Stability: Elite Responses to Political Conflict* [New York: Wiley, 1976], p. 164.) Tapper is not clear as to whether blacks may have been reacting to their relatively deprived condition in the early 1960s, or to their improving conditions during the mid-1960s. Tapper's thesis should certainly be considered seriously, although, as we have seen, feelings of social deprivation among black schoolchildren do not seem to contribute to feelings of political powerlessness or to political distrust (see pp. 52–53).

Chapter 5.   The Intelligence Explanation

David Easton and Robert D. Hess's study of 12,000 American schoolchildren suggested that, apart from age, intelligence was the best predictor of sense of political efficacy. Children with high IQ scores were much more likely to feel politically efficacious than those with medium IQ scores, and children with medium IQs felt much more efficacious than those with low IQ scores.[1] In their study of 398 Honolulu high school students, Susan K. Harvey and Ted G. Harvey also found intelligence to be positively related to high political efficacy, although this relationship was weak.[2] Abundant data show that black children tend to score lower on intelligence tests than do white children. Although within-race differences in measured intelligence are much greater than between-race differences, the latter are substantial, usually about 15 points, or one standard deviation.[3] Given the importance of discussions of intelligence in the political socialization literature, and given the between-race differences in measured intelligence, we should explore the possibility that the low levels of political effectiveness among blacks might result from their lower mean intelligence.

The following assumptions constitute the intelligence explanation:

Assumption C.1. Low levels of intelligence contribute to low feelings of political effectiveness.

Assumption C.2. Blacks tend to be less intelligent than whites.

As we shall soon see, there is very little support for either of these assumptions.

Assumption C.2. Although, for our purposes, Assumption C.2 is a lower level assumption than Assumption C.1, we will discuss C.2 first, for the logical status of the intelligence explanation depends upon our interpretation of the low mean intelligence scores among black children.

To some extent, the lower measured intelligence of blacks may result from the cultural biases of intelligence tests. Tests are written in standard middle-class English, and sometimes include questions tapping knowledge that white children are more likely to learn than blacks. The evidence about "culture-free" tests, or tests biased in favor of blacks, is not consistent, but some of the mean difference between blacks and whites probably results from biases in the tests most frequently used to measure intelligence.[4] To the extent that available tests do not validly measure intelligence, Assumption C.2 may be unsupported.

Let us suppose that intelligence tests do measure those problem-solving abilities that laymen often call "intelligence," but that for reasons unrelated to intelligence black children do not perform well. Black children may perceive a world of restricted opportunity in which their intelligence scores are unrelated to their life-chances. Black children may feel threatened by tests designed and administered by whites. That black children often score higher on intelligence tests when they are administered by blacks, suggests that their low scores are at least partly spurious.[5] Once again, we must question Assumption C.2.

Suppose that low intelligence scores of blacks are true scores, and that black children do not have the intellectual abilities to score well. But let us also suppose that this lack of ability results from their restricted opportunity and low accorded respect. In other words, let us assume that the environmentalists are correct, and that the low scores of black children result from their social environment. Intelligence would then become an intervening variable between social structure and political attitudes. The intelligence explanation might be valid, but it could be incorporated into the social-deprivation explanation, so long as we specified that intelligence was an intervening psychological variable. Intelligence might join self-confidence as an intervening variable although, as we will see, the two are probably interrelated. But there is a fundamental difference between intelligence and self-confidence. No one claims that the latter is genetically determined.

The intelligence explanation assumes an independent status if we accept the view that racial differences in intelligence are genetically based.[6] Intelligence, in this view, precedes social structure, and the intelligence explanation becomes independent of the social-deprivation explanation. The logical status of the intelligence explanation becomes more complex if we conclude that racial differences in intelligence result from differences in nutrition, or from differences in prenatal care.[7] Racial differences in intelligence would then result from social deprivation, but intelligence would precede the restricted opportunity and denied respect that impede the development of self-confidence.

Evaluating the current controversies about the relationship between race and intelligence would probably lead us to consider intelligence as an intervening variable that might stand between the social-structural conditions that deprive blacks and the political attitudes of black schoolchildren. In other words, few would contend that racial differences in measured intelligence result solely from cultural biases in the measurement instrument or from black children not trying to score well. But there seems to be abundant evidence that the low scores among blacks result largely from environmental factors.[8] However, the debate over race and intelligence is quite complex (and beyond my own area of expertise). But we do not need to sort out these arguments, for the intelligence explanation can be discarded by examining the assumptions that link intelligence to feelings of political competence.

Assumption C.1. Low levels of intelligence contribute to low feelings of political effectiveness.

The intelligence explanation assumes that certain cognitive capacities contribute to feelings of political effectiveness. Persons with very limited intelligence cannot understand their political environment, and have little or no idea about methods of influencing political leaders. But once we go beyond a minimum (though admittedly unspecified) threshold, there remains little theoretical reason for expecting intelligence to contribute to feelings of political effectiveness.

Elliott S. White presents the most extensive arguments about why intelligence should contribute to feelings of political effectiveness among schoolchildren.[9] First, he argues, brighter children are better able to understand their environment, and are more likely to believe they can influence it. But this argument is questionable since children, regardless of their intelligence, have little or no power to influence political leaders. Second, White advances a "more socio-psychological" explanation. Intelligence scores may measure more than cognitive capacities, but also "certain general personality traits and attitudes which are a manifestation of the child's interaction with his environment."[10] White cites Harrison G. Gough, who argued that there were "personological correlates of general intelligence," first among which were "self-confidence and self-assurance."[11] But if measured intelligence is closely related to self-confidence (and if intelligence tests partly measure self-confidence), and if self-confidence is affected by social structures, then the intelligence explanation can be incorporated into the social-deprivation explanation.

Robert D. Hess and Judith V. Torney say little about why intelligence contributes to feelings of political effectiveness. They do note that brighter children "are more completely socialized in political attitudes and behavior" by grade eight than less intelligent children are.[12] Presumably, they consider political efficacy to be a norm, and intelligent children are more likely to learn it. David Easton and Jack

Dennis argue that intelligent children are more likely to learn the "regime norm" of political efficacy.[13] In addition, they argue a brighter child is more likely to have a high sense of "general confidence," and is more likely to believe he can cope with his environment. "From this perspective," they write, "his feeling that the ordinary member of the political system has influence is a natural accompaniment of his own greater ego strength and trust in his capacity to deal with the world."[14] If this second formulation is correct, the intelligence explanation can be incorporated into the social-deprivation explanation.

Assuming there are theoretical reasons for intelligence to contribute to feelings of political effectiveness, we must scrutinize the empirical finding that intelligence and sense of political efficacy are strongly related. White's analysis was methodologically unsound for, as he acknowledged later, he used inappropriate statistical techniques.[15] Hess and Torney and Easton and Dennis used correct techniques to evaluate the explanatory power of measured intelligence, but both sets of authors overlooked a major methodological problem.

Intelligence data on children were obtained directly from school records, whereas the children themselves provided data about their social background. Data on social class, for example, were compiled from responses to a closed-ended question in which children were asked to describe their father's job. The job descriptions employed, which were later used to classify students, do not neatly fit standard sociological classifications of occupational rankings.[16] Moreover, information obtained from schoolchildren, and especially from children in the early grades, may be less reliable than information about intelligence quotients obtained directly from school records.[17] Since measured intelligence may be one of the most reliable measures employed by Easton and Hess,[18] we would expect it to have greater explanatory power than socioeconomic data obtained from schoolchildren. There is a clear relationship between measured intelligence and feelings of political effectiveness. But the relative strength of that relationship, compared with other relationships in the Easton-Hess study, may result partially from the better measurement techniques used to assess intelligence.

The Harvey and Harvey study also raises methodological problems. Though they carefully discuss the problems of reliability and validity in measuring intelligence, they provide little information about their measure of socioeconomic status.[19] Nevertheless, they found that the weak positive relationship between intelligence and feelings of political effectiveness was eliminated when they introduced controls for socioeconomic status.[20]

In summary, there is little theoretical and somewhat questionable empirical support for Assumption C.1. Nevertheless, if we did accept the intelligence explanation it would lead to one additional empirical consequence.

Empirical Consequence C.1. Among black children, those with high intelligence scores should feel more politically efficacious than those with low intelligence scores. Controlling for intelligence should reduce or eliminate racial differences in sense of political effectiveness.

I do not argue that such a relationship exists, only that it would exist if the intelligence explanation were valid. But even if high intelligence contributes to feelings of political efficacy among whites, it would not necessarily contribute to high efficacy among blacks. For if blacks are deprived of political power, intelligent blacks might be more likely to recognize this powerlessness than less intelligent blacks, and thus might have lower feelings of political effectiveness.

Unfortunately, there are scant data with which to test this thesis. In my review of the extant political socialization literature, I found only two studies of political efficacy that used measures of intelligence among black schoolchildren, and they yielded contradictory results. Edward G. Carmines' study of 224 black and 197 white junior high school students, conducted in Hampton, Virginia, in the spring of 1971 (see Appendix A), found a positive correlation between intelligence scores and feelings of political effectiveness among blacks (Pearson's r = .20), although that relationship was stronger among whites (.32).[21] Since whites had higher IQ scores than blacks, controlling for IQ scores reduced the zero-order relationship between race and feelings of political efficacy. Whereas the zero-order relationship between race and political efficacy was -.14, it fell to -.06 when controls for intelligence scores were introduced.[22]

Carmines argues that racial differences in intelligence can explain the low feelings of political efficacy among black schoolchildren. "Why," he asks, "are the black students less efficacious than the whites?" He answers, "Although there are many reasonable responses to this inquiry, the one supported by this study is that the difference in sense of political efficacy between black and white students can be largely explained by the racial differences in intelligence. That is, when intelligence is held constant, the black students are hardly any less efficacious than the whites."[23] However, Carmines' conclusion is also compatible with the social-deprivation explanation, for, as he adds, "It should also be noted that the racial difference in IQ probably reflects the environmental advantage that whites have in relation to blacks in the United States."[24]

But while Carmines' study supports Empirical Consequence C.1, Thomas S. Grotelueschen's study does not. Grotelueschen's survey of fifth- through eighth-grade blacks in Alachua County and in Jacksonville, Florida, conducted in late 1971 and early 1972, found intelligence negatively related to feelings of political effectiveness. Grotelueschen divided children into three categories: IQs of 100 or more, IQs between 85 and 99, and IQs of 84 and below, and there were 145, 148, and 142 blacks in each category, respectively.[25] He then used a five-item index to measure feelings of political effectiveness, employing the same items used by Easton and Dennis (and by Carmines). Blacks with high and medium intelligence scores had slightly *lower* feelings of political effectiveness than those with low intelligence scores. (Mean scores were: high IQ blacks = 2.6; medium IQ blacks = 2.6; low IQ blacks = 2.9).[26] While these differences were not statistically significant, the slight negative relationship between measured intelligence and feelings of political efficacy (or even the absence of a positive relationship) tends to undermine the intelligence explanation.

HARRELL R. RODGERS, JR.'S, TEST OF THE INTELLIGENCE EXPLANATION

Rodgers performed an indirect test of the intelligence explanation, although he recognized that it was weak theoretically. "As Abramson points out," he wrote, "on theoretical grounds the explanation seems to make more sense for white children than black, since the brighter a black student is, the more likely he would be to realize that political advantage in the United States is weighted on the side of whites."[27] Moreover, because he had serious reservations about the validity of IQ tests for blacks, Rodgers chose a measure of school achievement based upon grade average. (In fact, Rodgers had little choice but to use an indirect measure of intelligence, since the schools he studied did not use standard IQ tests.) Rodgers found a slight tendency for black students with high grades to feel less politically efficacious than those with low grades. For whites, on the other hand, school achievement related positively to feelings of political efficacy. Rodgers found that among blacks the negative relationship between school achievement and feelings of political efficacy disappeared when controls for social position were introduced, whereas among whites the positive relationship was not affected by such controls.[28] These data suggest that high intelligence may contribute to feelings of political effectiveness among whites, but not among blacks.

Unfortunately, Rodgers' test is too indirect. School achievement is probably related to intelligence for IQ scores, if nothing else, are usually good predictors of academic success. But school achievement is affected by many factors other than intelligence. Moreover, even if Rodgers were skeptical of the validity of IQ scores for blacks, his test would have been stronger if he had been able to supplement his grade score measure with actual IQ scores. Last, it should be remembered that Schley R. Lyons, who also used school achievement (which he considered an indirect measure of self-confidence), found a positive relationship between achievement and feelings of political effectiveness among black schoolchildren.[29]

EVALUATION OF THE INTELLIGENCE EXPLANATION

The intelligence explanation has only weak theoretical and questionable empirical support, and the basic additional empirical consequence that follows from it received little support. But it is questionable whether, even in principle, it can account for racial differences in political trust. One could argue that persons with low intelligence should be more trusting than highly intelligent persons (unless intelligence scores are surrogate measures of self-confidence). Persons with low cognitive capacities might be less capable of finding fault with their political leaders, whereas intelligent persons might recognize that leaders can be both dishonest and incompetent. On the other hand, an intelligent person might recognize that, although leaders are occasionally dishonest, they are more often honest. He might be more likely to learn the norm that political leaders in a democracy are usually trustworthy.

Not only are the theoretical expectations about the relationship between intelligence and political trust ambiguous, there are also few studies relating intelligence to feelings of political trust. Hess and Torney and Easton and Dennis found intelligence to be only weakly and inconsistently related to benevolent attitudes toward authority, a finding consistent with our argument that one should expect no such relationship.[30] In his panel study of tenth-grade boys, Jerald G. Bachman found a positive, but weak, relationship between intelligence and trust in government.[31] Grotelueschen found a slight positive relationship between intelligence and trust and political trust among the blacks he surveyed, but the relationship was not significant.[32] And both Rodgers and Lyons found school achievement to be weakly related to political trust.[33] At best, then, the intelligence explanation is essentially silent about Finding 2.

NOTES

1. Robert D. Hess and Judith V. Torney, *The Development of Political Attitudes in Children* (Chicago: Aldine, 1967), pp. 149–152; David Easton and

Jack Dennis, "The Child's Acquisition of Regime Norms: Political Efficacy," *American Political Science Review,* 61 (March 1967), pp. 25–38, at pp. 34–35.

2. S. K. Harvey and T. G. Harvey, "Adolescent Political Outlooks: The Effects of Intelligence as an Independent Variable," *Midwest Journal of Political Science,* 14 (November 1970), pp. 565–595, at pp. 585–587.

3. For an extensive summary of findings about racial differences in measured intelligence, see John C. Loehlin, Gardner Lindzey, and J. N. Spuhler, *Race Differences in Intelligence* (San Francisco: Freeman, 1975), pp. 164–195.

4. For a summary of these findings, see *ibid.,* pp. 64–72.

5. See Herman G. Canady, "The Effect of 'Rapport' on the I.Q.: A New Approach to the Problem of Racial Psychology," *Journal of Negro Education,* 5 (April 1936), pp. 209–219; and E. Earl Baughman and W. Grant Dalhstrom, *Negro and White Children: A Psychological Study in the Rural South* (New York: Academic Press, 1968), pp. 39–40.

6. Arthur R. Jensen is the main proponent of this view. See his "How Much Can We Boost IQ and Scholastic Achievement?," *Harvard Educational Review,* 39 (Winter 1969), pp. 1–123, and his *Educability and Group Differences* (New York: Harper and Row, 1972). In Britain, the main proponent of this view is Hans J. Eysenck. See his *The IQ Argument: Race, Intelligence and Education* (New York: Library Press, 1971).

7. See Loehlin, Lindzey, and Spuhler, *Race Differences in Intelligence,* pp. 196–229, for a discussion of the effects of nutrition.

8. See Otto Klineberg, *Negro Intelligence and Selective Migration* (New York: Columbia University Press, 1935); Melvin M. Tumin, ed., *Race and Intelligence* (New York: Anti-Defamation League of B'nai B'rith, 1963); Thomas F. Pettigrew, *A Profile of the American Negro* (Princeton, N.J.: Van Nostrand, 1964), pp. 100–135; Lee J. Cronbach, "Heredity, Environment, and Educational Policy," *Harvard Educational Review,* 39 (Spring 1969), pp. 338–347; and Arthur L. Stinchcombe, "Environment: The Cumulation of Effects Is Yet to Be Understood," *Harvard Educational Review,* 39 (Summer 1969), pp. 511–522.

Other scholars, while not denying the possibility of genetic differences, conclude that Jensen's calculations about the relative contribution of genetic effects to racial differences in intelligence are fundamentally unsound. See W. F. Bodmer, "Race and IQ: The Genetic Background," in *Race, Culture and Intelligence,* eds. Ken Richardson and David Spears (Harmondsworth, Middlesex: Penguin, 1972), pp. 83–113; Richard C. Lewontin, "Race and Intelligence," *Bulletin of the Atomic Scientists,* 26 (March 1970), pp. 2–8; and David Layzer, "Heritability Analyses of IQ Scores: Science or Numerology?", *Science,* 183 (29 March 1974), pp. 1259–1266.

9. Elliott S. White, "Intelligence and Sense of Political Efficacy in Children," *Journal of Politics,* 30 (August 1968), pp. 710–731, and "Intelligence, Individual Differences and Learning: An Approach to Political Socialization," *British Journal of Sociology,* 20 (March 1969), pp. 50–68. White extends these arguments in "Genetic Diversity and Political Life: Toward a Populational-Interaction Paradigm," *Journal of Politics,* 34 (November 1972), pp. 1203–1242.

10. White, "Intelligence and Sense of Political Efficacy," p. 722.

11. See Harrison G. Gough, "A Nonintellectual Intelligence Test," *Journal of Consulting Psychology,* 17 (August 1953), pp. 242–246.

12. Hess and Torney, *The Development of Political Attitudes,* p. 129.

13. Easton and Dennis, "The Child's Acquisition of Regime Norms," p. 34.

14. *Ibid.,* pp. 34–35.

15. As Robert W. Jackman points out, White interpreted tests of statistical significance as a measure of the strength of the relationship between intelligence and feelings of political efficacy. (See Jackman, "A Note on Intelligence, Social Class, and Political Efficacy in Children," *Journal of Politics,* 32 [November 1970], pp. 984–989.) White acknowledged that his methodology was inappropriate. (See "The Author Responds," *Journal of Politics,* 32 [November 1970], pp. 992–993.) See also Fred I. Greenstein, "The Standing of Social and Psychological Variables: An Addendum to Jackman's Critique," *Journal of Politics,* 32 (November 1970), pp. 989–992.

16. The main problem is the intermediate category (code category 3) employed by Easton and Hess that combines office workers, salesmen, owners of small stores, and government workers. (See Hess and Torney, *The Development of Basic Attitudes and Values Toward Government and Citizenship During the Elementary School Years, Part 1,* Report to U.S. Office of Education on Cooperative Project No. 1078 [Chicago: University of Chicago, 1965], p. 486). The large number of jobs included in this category cover a wide range of occupational levels, as can be seen by examining the occupational ranking system developed by Peter M. Blau and Otis Dudley Duncan. See Blau and Duncan, *The American Occupational Structure* (New York: Wiley, 1967), pp. 122–123.

17. As Richard G. Niemi demonstrated through his analysis of the 1965 SRC survey of high school students and their parents, seniors who were individually interviewed by trained field interviewers provided fairly reliable information about their father's occupation. (See Niemi, *How Family Members Perceive Each Other: Political and Social Attitudes in Two Generations* [New Haven, Conn.: Yale University Press, 1974], pp. 23–27.) However, the Easton and Hess data about political efficacy were collected from third through eighth graders in a mass-administered paper-and-pencil questionnaire.

18. As the Easton and Hess study included only whites, the special problems of reliability and validity faced when using IQ tests among blacks were not encountered.

19. Harvey and Harvey, "Adolescent Political Outlooks," pp. 569–575.

20. *Ibid.,* p. 591.

21. Edward G. Carmines, "Race, Intelligence and Sense of Political Efficacy: A Multivariate Political Socialization Study," unpublished M.A. thesis, College of William and Mary, 1972, pp. 72–73. IQ was measured by the Verbal California Test of Mental Maturity, and the scores were obtained from school records.

22. *Ibid.,* p. 73.

23. *Ibid.,* pp. 76–77.

24. *Ibid.,* p. 77.

25. Thomas S. Grotelueschen, "The Political Orientations of Black Children in Northern Florida," unpublished Ph.D. dissertation, University of Wisconsin, 1973, pp. 56–57. Grotelueschen also obtained IQ scores from school records, but did not report the type of IQ test employed.

26. *Ibid.,* p. 66. Scores on his index ranged from 1.0 to 5.0.

27. Harrell R. Rodgers, Jr., "Toward Explanation of the Political Efficacy and Political Cynicism of Black Adolescents: An Exploratory Study," *American Journal of Political Science,* 18 (May 1974), pp. 257–282, at p. 272.

28. *Ibid.,* p. 273.

29. Schley R. Lyons, "The Political Socialization of Ghetto Children: Efficacy and Cynicism," *Journal of Politics,* 32 (May 1970), pp. 288–304, at pp. 299–301. See p. 46 above.

30. Hess and Torney, *The Development of Political Attitudes,* pp. 135–137; Easton and Dennis, *Children in the Political System: Origins of Political Legitimacy* (New York: McGraw-Hill, 1969), pp. 363–379.

31. Jerald G. Bachman, *Youth in Transition, Volume 2: The Impact of Family Background and Intelligence on Tenth-Grade Boys* (Ann Arbor, Mich.: Institute for Social Research, 1970), p. 209. Bachman did not report this relationship among his subset of black respondents.

32. Grotelueschen, "The Political Orientation of Black Children," p. 85. Carmines did not measure feelings of political trust.

33. Rodgers, "Toward Explanation," p. 273; Lyons, "The Political Socialization of Ghetto Children," p. 302. Rodgers reports this relationship only for blacks. Lyons did not present this relationship according to race.

Chapter 6. The Political-Reality Explanation

Political scientists have usually considered feelings of political effectiveness and trust to be largely a function of sociological or psychological attributes. They have less often considered ways such feelings might be affected by actual political power arrangements and by the trustworthiness of political leaders.[1] Yet we can argue that blacks have less political power than whites and that they have less reason to trust political leaders. Joan E. Laurence specifically, and Edward S. Greenberg more indirectly, argued that the political attitudes of black schoolchildren reflect an accurate response to the political realities that black Americans face.[2] Since my earlier version of this explanation was published, other political scientists have speculated that black children may be responding to political realities.[3]

The following assumptions constitute the political-reality explanation:

Assumption D.1. Blacks have less capacity to influence political leaders than whites have.

Assumption D.2. Political leaders are less trustworthy in their dealings with blacks than in their dealings with whites.

Assumption D.3. Black children know these facts, or they are indirectly influenced by adults who know these facts, or both.

Assumption D.1. That blacks are less politically powerful than whites may seem like a truism, but it is hard to measure political influence. Although only a few political leaders are black, blacks may effectively influence white political leaders. Certain decision rules, however, tend to minimize black political influence. Robert A. Dahl demonstrated that the decision rule that each state have two senators benefited certain groups, such as cotton farmers and silver miners, but weakened the influence of coal miners, wage earners, migrant farm workers, and blacks.[4] The congressional seniority system also tended to deprive blacks of political power.[5] On the other hand, the decision rule through which the president is selected may benefit blacks because many live in pivotal states with large numbers of electoral votes.[6]

The main limitation on black political influence is that they are a minority in a system governed by majority rule. Blacks may be part of a coalition of minorities, but they must always seek partners. These partners have helped them up to a point; yet, when the issues involve zero-sum conflicts that blacks can win only at the expense of whites, blacks are unlikely to win.

Assumption D.2. Political leaders are less trustworthy in their dealings with blacks than in their dealings with whites.

If blacks are deprived of political power, one may expect political leaders to be less trustworthy with blacks than with whites. A leader is more likely to be trustworthy when he is bargaining with persons and groups who have sanctions over him. To the extent that blacks are deprived of political power, they may be deprived of the resources necessary to keep political leaders honest.

Nonetheless, it is difficult to provide empirical support for Assumption D.2. Have political leaders broken promises made to blacks more often than those made to whites? Have they been more corrupt in their dealings with blacks than with whites? Have they been less competent? It would be difficult to answer empirically any of the above questions.

Assumption D.3. Black children know these facts, or they are indirectly influenced by adults who know these facts, or both.

Despite our difficulty supporting Assumptions D.1 and D.2, the political-reality explanation is compelling, for few knowledgeable observers would deny the veracity of these assumptions. The main problem with the explanation is that we are attempting to explain political attitudes among children. Children, unlike adults, have little opportunity to engage in reality testing with their political environment. Moreover, compared with adults, children lack political knowledge. Thus, even if we accept as factual that blacks are deprived of political power and have reason to distrust political leaders, we cannot assume that black children know these facts.

Few children, black or white, have a sophisticated understanding of political decision rules, or adequate knowledge to evaluate the trustworthiness of public officials. We have no reason to believe that black children are particularly sophisticated in such matters, for on tests of political knowledge black children have usually scored lower than white children.[7]

Perhaps black children are influenced indirectly by black adults who do know these facts. Although some local samples have found black adults to feel more efficacious than white adults,[8] national probability samples have consistently found blacks to feel less politically efficacious. The most impressive time-series data are provided by the Survey Research Center of the University of Michigan, which has asked four basic efficacy questions from 1952 on.[9] As the data in Table 6-1 show, in all nine surveys in which these items were used blacks have felt less efficacious than whites.[10] Racial differences were most pronounced in the 1950s and least marked in 1964.[11] Since 1964 feelings of political efficacy have declined on the first three items in the table, but the proportion who recognize ways other than voting to influence the government has increased.[12] For three of the items, "officials don't care," "so complicated," and "voting is the only way," racial differences were somewhat larger in 1974 than in 1964, but on the remaining item, "don't have any say," racial differences were identical (and small) in both years. On balance, although the sharp racial differences of the 1950s no longer obtain, overall levels of racial differences on these items have been remarkably consistent for the past two decades.

Racial differences in political trust, on the other hand, have changed quite dramatically. As the data in Table 6-2 show, the Michigan SRC data reveal a time-series trend that is similar to that found among schoolchildren. In 1958, when these items were first used, blacks were about as trusting as whites. Political trust among whites remained fairly stable between 1958 and 1964, but it rose among blacks, and in both 1964 and 1966 blacks were usually as trusting, or more trusting, than whites on most items. In 1968 political trust dropped among both races, and on the one item that directly asked whether the government in Washington could be trusted to do what is right, blacks were slightly less trusting than whites. In 1964 blacks had been more likely than whites to deny that government officials were crooked, but in 1968 racial differences on this item had been eliminated. In 1970 trust again dropped for both races, but the drop was far sharper among blacks than among whites. Blacks were now much more likely to say that political leaders were crooked, much less likely to say that government leaders in Washington could be trusted to do what is right, and less likely to say the government was run for the benefit of all. By 1972 blacks were less trusting than whites on four of the five questions asked, and for the first time were as likely as whites to say the government wastes a lot of tax money. By 1974, with the impact of Watergate, trust again dropped markedly among both races, but blacks were less trusting than whites on all five questions. That a similar time-series trend is found among both adults and children adds considerable credibility to the political-reality explanation. Still, it should be recognized that the most pronounced shift among black adults occured between 1968 and 1970, sometime after the time-series shift among schoolchildren.

But, however plausible the thesis may be, we have no direct evidence that the political attitudes among black adults are caused by changes in their political environment. Nor can we demonstrate that the political attitudes of black adults are transmitted to black schoolchildren. What limited evidence we have suggests that attitudes, such as feelings of political efficacy and cynicism, are not usually transmitted from parents to their children.[13] Dennis' study suggests that black children are less likely than white children to share their parents' feelings of political efficacy, and no more likely than white children to share their parents' evaluation of the trustworthiness of government officials.[14] Richard G. Niemi's analysis of the Michigan SRC survey of high school seniors and their parents showed blacks to be no more likely than whites to share their parents' feelings of political effectiveness although they were marginally more likely to share their parents' feelings of political cynicism.[15] Of course, black children could learn about political realities from adults other than their parents. The thesis that political values are transmitted from adults to children through a black political subculture is certainly consistent with the political-reality explanation, for blacks could learn about realities through this subcultural communications process.[16] However, we have no direct data about the communications process through which this subcultural socialization might operate.

Black children may learn about political realities directly through their contact with government officials like policemen and welfare workers. Perhaps black children learn to distrust these authorities and generalize this distrust toward other political authority figures. But Harrell R. Rodgers, Jr., and George Taylor's analysis suggests that black schoolchildren do not generalize distrust of policemen to other authority figures.[17] David O. Sears and John B. McConahay note that black children have consistently been much more negative toward the police than white children have, but they conclude that "this seems to be due more to the reality problems that blacks have with police . . . rather than to any lack of commitment to the political and authority system per se."[18] It should be noted that most of the items used by political socialization researchers (see Appendix C) have tapped trust toward national-level authority figures with whom neither white nor black schoolchildren are likely to have any direct contact.

Finally, we should ask whether black children must be influenced directly by political realities for the political-reality explanation to be valid. For example, black children may learn, through their day-to-day experiences, that whites cannot be trusted, and may then project this

TABLE 6-1   Percentage of Adults Who Felt Politically Efficacious from 1952 to 1974, by Race[a]

YEAR OF SURVEY	1952	1956	1960	1964	1966	1968	1970	1972	1974
Percentage who disagreed public officials don't care what people like me think, by race:									
Black[b]	39[c]	47	62	46	39	42	29	30	26
White	65	74	74	63	59	57	52	51	48
Percentage who disagreed people like me don't have any say about what the government does, by race:									
Black	42	44	60	65	49	48	52	53	53
White	70	74	73	70	62	59	66	60	58
Percentage who disagreed politics and government seem so complicated that a person like me can't really understand what's going on, by race:									
Black	17	19	35	30	16	20	23	19	20
White	30	38	42	32	28	30	27	27	27
Percentage who disagreed voting is the only way people like me can have any say about how the government runs things, by race:									
Black	7	12	12	13	16	20	22	22	17
White	18	26	26	27	28	45	42	39	40

[a]SOURCE: Surveys conducted by the Survey Research Center of the University of Michigan. The data were provided by the Inter-University Consortium for Political Research, which bears no responsibility for my analyses or interpretations.

The following four items were used:

I don't think public officials care much about what people like me think.   Agree   Disagree

People like me don't have any say about what the government does.   Agree   Disagree

Sometimes politics and government seem so complicated that a person like me can't really understand what's going on.   Agree   Disagree

Voting is the only way that people like me can have any say about how the government runs things.   Agree   Disagree

[b]Data for blacks in 1964, 1968, and 1970 include the black supplement.

[c]The numbers upon which these percentages are based vary slightly from item to item. The lowest number upon which they are based is as follows: 1952, 167 blacks, 1590 whites; 1956, 143 blacks, 1590 whites; 1960, 157 blacks (weighted N), 1717 whites (weighted N); 1964, 415 blacks, 1387 whites; 1966, 135 blacks, 1137 whites; 1968, 235 blacks (weighted N), 1188 whites; 1970, 280 blacks (weighted N), 1391 whites; 1972, 263 blacks, 2386 whites; 1974, 217 blacks (weighted N), 2231 whites (weighted N).

TABLE 6-2 Percentage of Adults Who Trusted the Government from 1958 to 1974, by Race[a]

YEAR OF SURVEY	1958	1964	1966	1968	1970	1972	1974
Percentage who said the government in Washington can be trusted to do what is right always or most of the time, by race:							
Black[b]	62[c]	74	64	58	36	31	18
White	74	77	65	61	55	56	38
Percentage who said the government wastes not much or only some tax money, by race:							
Black	55	69	—	56	40	30	14
White	52	49	—	37	29	33	24
Percentage who said people running the government are smart people who usually know what they are doing, by race:							
Black	47	71	—	57	37	43	36
White	58	68	—	58	53	56	50
Percentage who said hardly any or not many government officials are crooked, by race:							
Black	73	76	—	72	49	33	41
White	70	66	—	71	67	62	52
Percentage who said the government is run for the benefit of all, by race:							
Black	—	69	64	64	35	24	19
White	—	63	52	49	41	39	25

[a]SOURCE: Surveys conducted by the Survey Research Center of the University of Michigan. The data were provided by the Inter-University Consortium for Political Research, which bears no responsibility for my analyses or interpretations.

The following five questions were used:

How much of the time do you think you can *trust* the government in Washington to do what is right—*just about always, most of the time,* or *only some of the time?*

Do you think that people in the government waste *a lot* of the money we pay in taxes, waste *some* of it, or *don't waste very much of it?*

Do you feel that almost all of the people running the government are smart people who usually *know what they are doing,* or do you think that quite a few of them *don't seem to know what they are doing?*

Do you think that *quite a few* of the people running the government are a little crooked, *not very many are,* or do you think that *hardly any* of them are crooked at all?

Would you say the government is pretty much run by *a few big interests* looking out for themselves or that it is run for the *benefit of all* the people?

[b]Data for blacks in 1964, 1968, and 1970 include the black supplement.

[c]The numbers upon which these percentages are based vary slightly from item to item. The lowest number upon which they are based is as follows: 1958, 155 blacks (weighted N), 1598 whites (weighted N); 1964, 378 blacks, 1279 whites; 1966, 132 blacks, 1127 whites; 1968, 237 blacks (weighted N), 1181 whites; 1970, 280 blacks (weighted N), 1379 whites; 1972, 219 blacks, 2019 whites; 1974, 222 blacks (weighted N), 2225 whites (weighted N).

generalized knowledge to political leaders, most of whom they know are white. But such learning would best be accounted for by the social-deprivation explanation, for it is largely through the restriction of opportunity and denial of respect that blacks learn to distrust whites.

Even though we cannot spell out the processes through which black children may learn about political realities, the political-reality explanation leads to a series of empirical consequences that are supported by extant socialization research.

Empirical Consequence D.1. Feelings of political effectiveness and political trust should be lower among blacks who understand political realities than among those who do not.

Three studies allow us to test directly the relationship between political knowledge and political attitudes among black schoolchildren. Greenberg asked whether "whites and Negroes are treated the same."[19] Among black schoolchildren in Philadelphia, a "correct" perception that they were *not* was negatively related to political trust. Among black schoolchildren who said that Negroes and whites were not treated the same ($N = 162$), 45 per cent said the government in Washington could be trusted; among blacks who said they were treated the same ($N = 186$), 61 per cent trusted government officials.[20] Moreover, a "correct" perception of the way blacks were treated was also negatively related to appraisals of governmental competence. Among black children who said the races were treated differently, 29 per cent said the government almost never made mistakes, while among blacks who said they were treated the same, 51 per cent said the government almost never erred.[21] Of course, a child's perception about how the races are treated is not just a question of fact: his or her response may also tap beliefs about governmental and societal fairness. Thus, it could be argued that Greenberg's data do not support Empirical Consequence D.1, but merely show that responses to a given trust item are related to responses to two other trust items.

Harrell R. Rodgers, Jr., found that among black high school students in North Carolina political cynicism increased slightly with political knowledge (as measured by a four-item index),[22] although knowledge had no effect on feelings of political effectiveness.[23] Further analysis showed that political knowledge related positively to cynicism among blacks who had taken a civics course, and negatively among those who had not.[24] Participation in a civics course tended to raise the political cynicism of blacks in both segregated and integrated schools.[25] Rodgers also found that taking a civics course correlated with low feelings of political effectiveness among blacks in integrated schools. He concluded, "In integrated schools the civics course provides the student with new insights into restriction on black participation or citizen participation in general."[26]

Finally, Samuel Long developed two measures to assess the views of St. Louis high school students on the role of blacks in the political system.[27] A scale for perceived black political inefficacy measured the extent to which the respondent believed blacks lacked political influence. A scale for perceived black political distrust measured the extent to which the respondent believed that blacks had reason to distrust political leaders.[28] Long also developed three measures of the respondent's own feelings of political powerlessness and distrust.[29] Among blacks there was a strong relationship between feelings of perceived black political inefficacy and perceived black political distrust and individual feelings of political powerlessness and cynicism.[30] Long concluded that among black adolescents "perceptions of political reality do correlate with feelings of political alienation."[31]

Both Rodgers and Long concluded that their analyses supported the political-reality explanation. However, there are problems with both sets of tests, and they will be discussed more extensively below.[32]

Empirical Consequence D.2. Racial differences in feelings of political efficacy should be reduced or reversed in settings where blacks have political power.

In Chapter One, I cited James T. Jones' finding that in Gary, Indiana, whites were more likely than blacks to agree that "people like me and my parents don't have any say about what the government of our city does." Jones' explanation for this finding is consistent with the political-reality explanation: "The whites of Gary are outnumbered by Negroes, Negroes are very active politically, [and] there is a larger percentage of whites who are Republicans in a city dominated by the Democratic party."[33]

However, we have no reason to believe that blacks were politically advantaged in the three other settings where they were marginally more efficacious than whites: Pontiac, Michigan; Edgecombe County, North Carolina; and St. Louis, Missouri. But Rodgers argues that the whites in his North Carolina sample had reason to feel politically inefficacious. "We suspect," he writes, "that civil rights activities have embittered many whites who resent any progress in racial equality, and substantial numbers of blacks who feel that too little progress has been made."[34]

Empirical Consequence D.3. Blacks should be more trusting toward political leaders who depend upon black electoral support than toward leaders who do not rely on black support.

The decision rules for electing the president give blacks more influence than those for electing most public officials. Democratic presidential candidates, in particular, have relied heavily on black support.[35] And presidents, especially Democrats, have been more sympathetic to black demands than most other elected political leaders. It follows, then, that blacks should support the president, especially when he is a Democrat.

This empirical consequence is borne out by extant socialization research. Roberta S. Sigel found that black children in metropolitan Detroit expressed more concern over President Kennedy's death than white children did.[36] In a study conducted among Detroit area school-children in 1965, Dean Jaros found no racial differences in beliefs about presidential benevolence.[37] Henry I. Penfield's study of Alabama schoolchildren, conducted in February through May 1967, found that blacks were much more likely to have favorable attitudes toward the president than white children had.[38] In a study conducted in Philadelphia and Pittsburgh in the spring of 1968, Greenberg found black children to be only marginally less supportive of the president than white children were.[39] Merton S. Krause's study of Chicago-area schoolchildren, conducted in April and May of 1968, found no significant racial differences in feelings of political efficacy, trust, or duty toward the president.[40] Alden J. Stevens' study of Maryland children in May 1968 found blacks to score only marginally lower than whites on a presidential benevolence scale.[41] And Thomas J. Williams' study of Georgia schoolchildren, conducted in the spring of 1968, found that blacks were much less critical of the job Johnson was doing than white children were. Yet whites were more likely to praise the job Goldwater might have done if he had been elected.[42] "These data," Williams concludes, "support the theory of political reality proffered by Abramson to explain low levels of political trust among blacks.[43]

More recent data suggest that black children do not support the presidency *per se*, for they were more critical of Nixon than whites. Pauline Marie Vaillancourt's panel survey of San Francisco Bay area schoolchildren is particularly instructive.[44] She found that blacks were somewhat less likely to trust the president in December 1968, during Johnson's lame-duck presidency. In late January 1969, after Nixon's inauguration, trust dropped markedly among blacks, while rising slightly among whites. Racial differences were pronounced. By May and June of 1969, trust had dropped further among blacks, but it also fell among whites. Nonetheless, racial differences were still strong, with blacks much less trusting of the president than whites. A similar pattern emerged on two items that Vaillancourt considered measures of "attachment to the president," whether the respondent liked the president, and whether the president was "my favorite of all." Blacks were marginally less likely to like the president in late 1968, but were somewhat more likely to consider him their favorite. Both blacks and whites were less attached to Nixon than to Johnson, but in both 1969 surveys blacks were much less likely to like the president than white children were, and blacks were less likely to consider the president a "favorite."[45]

David O. Sears' data, collected in Fresno, California, in February 1971 also showed blacks to be less supportive of the president. Admittedly, as the data in Appendix A show, blacks were only somewhat more likely than whites to believe the president made mistakes. But blacks were much more likely to dislike Nixon than white children were, and black children were over twice as likely as white children to say the president wanted to help rich people more than poor people.[46] Anthony M. Orum and Roberta S. Cohen's study of Illinois schoolchildren, conducted in the spring and fall of 1971, also found black children to be less supportive of the president than white children were. Orum and Cohen developed a three-item presidential image scale, finding that at every grade level, and with social class controlled, blacks were less favorable to the president than whites.[47]

Harold M. Barger's survey of San Antonio elementary school children, conducted in the spring of 1973, further supports the trend. Barger found that blacks were less likely to believe the president was very honest than white children were.[48] They were also less likely to believe the president was a nice person or to like him.[49] However, in a survey conducted a year later (which also included middle school and high school students), positive affect toward the president had dropped markedly among white children. Positive affect fell among blacks as well, but it was already so low in 1973 that it had little room to fall. In 1974 blacks were still less supportive of the president than whites, although racial differences had been reduced.[50] Lorn S. Foster's study of East St. Louis and Peoria, Illinois, schoolchildren, conducted in March and May of 1974, provides additional evidence. Seventy-six per cent of the black schoolchildren said the president was less honest than most men, while only 40 per cent of the white children held this view.[51]

Among the questionnaire-based studies conducted since the end of the Johnson presidency, only two run counter to this general trend of low black support. Dean Jaros and Kenneth L. Kolson's study of rural communities near Middlefield, Ohio, conducted in May 1971, surveyed a small number of blacks, as well as Amish and non-Amish whites. Blacks were more likely to believe the president was honest than were non-Amish whites, but they were less trusting than the Amish.[52] On other measures of support for the president, blacks differed little from non-Amish whites, while being consistently less positive than the Amish. Jaros and Kolson emphasize, however, that their sample was highly atypical.[53] Richard C. Remy's study of high school seniors who had been selected to attend a nongovernmental training program in Washington, D.C., in the winter of 1971, found blacks to be only slightly less likely to agree that "when the going gets tough, the President can be trusted to level with the American people."[54] Remy, like Jaros and Kolson, emphasizes the atypical nature of his sample.[55]

Finally, we may note Fred I. Greenstein's study of ten- to fourteen-year-old school children conducted from mid-1969 to mid-1970 in Connecticut, eastern Pennsylvania, and upstate New York, for although he surveyed only 86 whites and 25 blacks he relied upon open-ended procedures. Children were asked to describe to a child from another country what the president does. Whereas 55 per cent of the white children manifested positive responses toward the president, only 32 per cent of the black children did.[56] Greenstein repeated these questions with 59 white Connecticut seventh-graders in June 1973, during the Senate Watergate hearings. Positive affect for the president had dropped to 45 per cent;[57] nonetheless, white children were still more supportive of the president than black children had been early in the Nixon presidency. Because of the small number of blacks interviewed, we must treat Greenstein's findings with caution, but his research suggests that alternative research strategies may yield similar racial differences in presidential affect.

The data suggest that black support for the president should not be viewed as support for the institution of the presidency, but is focused on the role incumbent. I am not suggesting that black children understand the decision rules that give blacks influence in electing presidents, and which give them considerable influence when he is a Democrat. Nor can I show that black children recognize that Democratic presidents have tended to support black demands. A more reasonable possibility is that black children learned their positive attitudes toward the president from black adults who did know that Kennedy and Johnson supported black demands, and that they learned their negative attitudes toward Nixon from black adults who recognized that he largely ignored them. It is also possible that black attitudes toward the president over this period were partly a function of their Democratic partisan loyalties, as well as the Democratic loyalties of black adults. In any event, these findings about black attitudes toward the president would be predicted by the political-reality explanation.

DISCUSSIONS OF THE
POLITICAL-REALITY EXPLANATION

David O. Sears, as we saw, evaluated the social-deprivation explanation, and concluded that the relationships it suggested had not been carefully documented by extant socialization research. Sears also discusses a simple social learning process that might account for racial differences in feelings of political efficacy and trust.[58] "The core of the social learning approach," he writes, "is that the organism incorporates environmental stimuli into itself as response dispositions in some simple, straightforward fashion. The basic proposition is that the child's political dispositions will be a more or less simple function of (1) environmental input and (2) the residues of previous learning." Sears explicitly rejects complex social learning formulations, arguing that "loving care for the arid esoterica of various learning approaches is hardly required for the crude levels of explanation political socialization researchers will be dealing with in the foreseeable future." He is far more sympathetic toward the political-reality explanation, for several indirect tests (based upon support for Empirical Consequences D.1, D.2, and D.3) "suggest that lesser efficacy and trust among black children are determined in an important way by their contact with political realities." The important point to stress is that these tests of the Empirical Consequences provide only indirect support for the political-reality explanation. They do not tell us how children learn about political realities or how such knowledge contributes to feelings of political powerlessness and distrust.

After evaluating alternative approaches to the study of children's attachments to the political system, Sears concludes that a simple social learning approach most closely fits the data. Moreover, social learning theory "is clearly the simplest and most parsimonious." "It would seem desirable," Sears concludes,

> to first assess the impact of simple social learning upon children's political attachments, before going on to assess the contribution made by more complex psychological processes. In other words, perhaps we should ask first what attitudes the child would acquire if he were only sampling randomly from the informational environment around him, and *then* ask how he is distorting that environment due to his psychological needs or cognitive limitations. The social learning approach ought to be invoked to its limits, as the simplest and most powerful theory, until it is confronted with data it cannot handle. Only at that point does it seem necessary, to this writer, to invoke more complex processes. And as of now it is not apparent that such data yet exist.

Morris, like Sears, had reservations about the social-deprivation explanation, for he questioned whether the relationships it postulated actually existed. Morris also criticized the political-reality explanation. He notes that "Abramson concedes that although the political reality thesis appears highly plausible as an explanation of black-white differences in political attitudes, it is extremely difficult to link empirically children's political attitudes to the powerlessness experienced by their parents.[59] We do not know, in other words, how political realities are learned and how they affect attitudes. But, as Morris notes, empirical consequences do follow from the political-reality explanation, and these consequences "appear to be supported by some existing research."[60]

Morris clearly favors a "subcultural theory." "A broader basis for explaining black-white differences in political attitudes and one that subsumes the social deprivation and political reality theories is the 'subculture theory.'"[61] Morris specifically refers to the explanation developed by Orum and Cohen. According to these authors, a subcultural socialization thesis suggests that children learn attitudes taught by their parents, peers, and schools, while the latter "transmit values which are part of a subculture within the larger society."[62] A subcultural explanation suggests that attitudinal similiarities between black youths and adults "occur partly because blacks both young and old are exposed to the values of the larger black subculture, and partly because black parents transmit such values to their children."[63]

Unfortunately, Orum and Cohen have no data on parental attitudes and, as we have seen, direct comparisons of parent-child pairs provide little evidence that black parents transmit attitudes such as political efficacy and political trust to their children.[64] Nor did Orum and Cohen have direct data on the extent to which a child was integrated into the black subculture—for example, the extent to which he received communications from blacks rather than whites. Their test of the subcultural explanation is based upon an attitudinal measure designed to tap the child's identification with the black community.[65] They found that black children who strongly identified with the black community were more politically cynical than blacks with low scores on their black consciousness scale.[66]

The subcultural socialization thesis is fully compatible with the political-reality explanation. The Orum and Cohen test shows that black children who are highly politicized as blacks are more likely to be politically cynical. The concept of subcultural socialization is potentially helpful for it suggests a process through which knowledge about political realities may be transmitted through the black community. But Orum and Cohen's explanation in no way "subsumes" either the social-deprivation explanation or the political-reality explanation and, unlike Morris, they make no claim that it does.[67]

The subcultural explanation has little relationship to the social-deprivation explanation. Why would black children who identify with the black community have low levels of self-confidence? We would expect the reverse to be true. Moreover, the subcultural thesis does not tell us why blacks feel less politically efficacious and trusting than whites do, whereas the political-reality explanation argues that these feelings are based upon black political powerlessness and the low trustworthiness of political leaders toward blacks. It is because of these political realities that the subcultural norms of political powerlessness and cynicism develop.

The subcultural explanation also needs greater development. Blacks are, after all, part of the American culture, and black children receive many communications from the mainstream culture—especially through the mass media. They also receive other mainstream information from the school. Black adults also receive many cues from the overall mass culture. Where does the mainstream culture end and the subculture begin? In addition, the subcultural explanation, as developed, does not tell us much about the actual communications processes through which subcultural norms are learned. Nonetheless, the Orum and Cohen thesis clearly merits further testing. And we must agree with Morris, "Much more rigorous and extensive test of the subculture theory is required, but it appears reasonable to conclude that the tradition of inferiority, deprivation, and oppression are crucial in shaping black political attitudes and values."[68]

TESTS OF THE POLITICAL-REALITY EXPLANATION

Rodgers found little support for the first three explanations, but he claimed to find considerable support for the fourth. Rodgers began his test by demonstrating that feelings of political efficacy and political trust were highly related, and argued that the strong relationship between these attitudinal variables showed that these feelings "reflect political antecedents."[69]

Rodgers could not test Assumption D.1 and D.2, although he was sensitive to the political realities of Edgecombe County. But his discussion of the powerlessness of blacks and whites is largely impressionistic, and the questions he used to measure political efficacy and cynicism tapped attitudes toward national-level authorities. Nor did Rodgers directly test Assumption D.3. Rather, he focused on testing Empirical Consequence D.1, that "feelings of political effectiveness and political trust should be lower among blacks who understand political realities than among those who do not." Rodgers concluded that he had found considerable support for this proposition, but his tests were often quite indirect.

Rodgers' most direct measure was a four-item index of political knowledge. Students were asked how many senators there were in the United States Senate, and the names of their governor, congressman, and mayor.[70] But this measure does not tap the extent to which blacks know about the political realities that deprive them of political power. Rodgers acknowledged that this measure was "not entirely satisfactory," but argued that "those students most attuned to the political system, and their position in it, would probably be the most likely to assimilate this type of information."[71] Rodgers' second measure was even more indirect: whether or not students had taken a civics course. Participation in a civics course was correlated with both political interest and political knowledge but, as Rodgers had no information about the content of these courses, he could not judge whether blacks who had taken them learned about the political realities faced by black Americans. It is not altogether clear why he relied so heavily on whether or not blacks had taken a civics course, although presumably he used this information as an indirect test of knowledge about political reality. We have already summarized Rodgers' findings.[72] but his conclusions depend largely on the assumption that knowing whether a black student has taken a civics course provides us with information about his knowledge of political realities. Rodgers maintains that his findings provided strong support for the political-reality explanation: "We conclude that the political efficacy and political cynicism of the black student does reflect political evaluations and that the political reality explanation provides important insight into the dependent variables."[73] It is important to recognize, however, that Rodgers reached this conclusion after conducting an indirect test of one empirical consequence of the explanation. Nor did Rodgers attempt to reconcile differences between his findings about the effects of the civics curriculum upon political efficacy with those obtained by Kenneth P. Langton and M. Kent Jennings in their national sample of high school seniors.[74]

Rodgers found additional support for the political-reality explanation when he examined the "environmental politicization" explanation developed by Kenneth P. Langton and David A. Karns. Langton and Karns speculated that "children reared in families where parents are interested in politics, discuss politics among themselves, and also participate in political activities, are more likely to have developed a sense of political efficacy than those students from less politicized families."[75] The environmental politicization explanation could account for low feelings of political efficacy among black children, when they come from less politicized families than white children do. Rodgers measured the level of discussion, as reported by the respondent, within the family, with friends outside of class, and with adults other than teachers.[76] However, he found no significant racial differences in levels of environmental politicization.[77] Nonetheless, Rodgers examined the relationship of political discussion to levels of political efficacy and trust. Among blacks, there were no significant relationships between political discussion and feelings of political efficacy. But blacks who discussed politics were a good deal more cynical than those who did not. Among blacks who discussed politics with their family several times a week, 43 per cent scored high on political cynicism, among those who never discussed politics with their family only 3 per cent did. Likewise, among blacks who frequently discussed politics with their peers, 44 per cent scored high on political cynicism, among those who did not discuss politics with their peers only 8 per cent did. "These findings," Rodgers concluded, "are supportive of the political reality explanation, since those black students who manifest the most interest and concern about politics (as reflected by the frequency of political discussions) are the most politically cynical."[78]

Rodgers continued his examination of the relationship between levels of political discussion and political cynicism by introducing controls for social status, but the direction of the relationship was altered in only one instance. Among blacks in the lower social strata, those who discussed politics with their families tended to be less cynical than those who did not. "These findings," Rodgers concluded, "might also be supportive of the political reality argument. For blacks with few social resources, an understanding of political reality does little to affect cynicism. But for those who might have the social resources to influence (or to have their parents influence) political leaders, an understanding of political reality erodes political trust."[79]

Rodgers' discussion of the effects of environmental politicization on political cynicism adds insight into the processes through which political realities may be learned. It suggests that black children who discuss politics with their parents and peers are more likely to become politically cynical than those who do not, strengthening the thesis that subcultural norms of political cynicism may pervade the black community. But, because we know nothing about the content of political discussion among blacks, Rodgers has provided only additional indirect evidence supporting Empirical Consequence D.1.

Throughout his entire analysis, Rodgers recognized the tentative nature of his conclusions, and almost always recognized those cases where his indicators were not adequate for a more direct test of the explanations. Rodgers emphasized the need for further research, and pointed to some directions it might take: "Studies of black political attitudes, especially those concerned with support for the political system, should be based on a theoretical framework which takes into consideration both political and psychological variables. More extensive efforts to determine how blacks evaluate the political activities of the government and their role in the political system should be especially rewarding."[80] Rodgers also reached another basic conclusion: "The data indicate . . .that only through alterations in the political fortunes of blacks can their feelings of political efficacy and political cynicism be shifted toward more supportive political attitudes."[81]

We may turn next to Samuel Long's evaluation of the political-reality explanation, which he tested with a survey of St. Louis inner-city high schools conducted in December 1974.[82] Long provided no test of Assumptions D.1 and D.2, and he did not discuss the political setting in St. Louis. While his data provide a partial test of Assumption D.3, he focused on examining Empirical Consequence D.1, by determining whether black children who understood political realities were less efficacious and trusting than those who did not.

The validity of Long's test depends upon his measure of perceptions of political reality. Two scales are crucial to his analysis, "a perceived black political inefficacy scale" and a "perceived black political distrust scale."[83] The former measures the extent to which the respondent believes that blacks are politically powerless,[84] the latter the extent to which the respondent believes that political leaders cannot be trusted in their dealings with blacks.[85] There were marked racial differences on these two measures. Black children were much more likely than white children to believe that blacks were politically powerless and were much more likely than whites to believe that blacks had reason to distrust political leaders.[86] If Long's scales are valid measures of perceptions of political reality, his data provide some support for Assumption D.3, for black students had some awareness of the political powerless of black Americans.

Long's test of the political reality explanation examined the separate effect of perceptions of reality on all four measures of political alienation—that is, on individual-level feelings of political inefficacy, discontentment, distrust, and estrangement. Long found that black students who believed that blacks were politically inefficacious and had reason to distrust political leaders were much more likely to feel alienated on all four of these individual-level measures.[87] (For example, a black who felt that blacks were politically powerless was more likely to feel that he was politically powerless as well.) Long also conducted a path analysis that simultaneously tested both the social-deprivation and the political-reality explanations with his St. Louis data.[88] He concluded that an integrated model combining both models was not useful because feelings of self-confidence were not strongly related to perceptions of political reality for either white or black adolescents. On the other hand, Long concluded that his data analysis provided consistent support for the hypotheses generated by the political-reality explanation.[89] Black students had markedly different views of political reality than white students had, and perceptions of political reality were strongly correlated with feelings of political alienation among black adolescents. "These data," Long concluded, "provide moderate support for the political reality model, especially as it applies to black adolescents."[90]

Our evaluation of Long's test depends upon whether or not we accept his measures of perceived black inefficacy and distrust. Long's questions did not test a student's knowledge of political facts but, rather, measured his evaluation of black political powerlessness and the extent to which he believed blacks had reason to distrust political leaders. Long measured opinions about the political status of blacks, whereas a better test would have tapped knowledge about actual political power arrangements that affect black Americans. He argues, by using a principal component factor analysis, that perceptions of black inefficacy and distrust form a separate attitudinal dimension from individual feelings of political efficacy and trust.[91] However, this principal component analysis was conducted for Long's total sample, including blacks and whites. Among whites, perceptions of black inefficacy and distrust were only weakly and inconsistently related to individual-level feelings of political efficacy and trust. By including whites in his principal component analysis, therefore, Long greatly increased the chances that perceptions about blacks and individual-level feelings would form separate dimensions.[92] Despite these criticisms, Long's test does provide considerable support for Empirical Consequence D.1, even though the test would have been stronger if he had included measures of perceptions of reality that directly measured factual information.

In his conclusion, Long recognizes some of the problems of the political-reality explanation. In the first place, he suggests that the relationship between perceptions and feelings may be multicausal. Although perceptions of reality may influence feelings of political efficacy and trust, feelings of efficacy and trust may also influence the way black children view political realities.[93] Second, Long maintains that some psychologists would not consider "perceptions" and "feelings" to be analytically distinct.[94] Last, Long argues that the reasons provided for the key linkages of the explanation are not adequate. Why, he asks, "must an adolescent who perceives the political system as being discriminatory, exploitive, and unresponsive hold feelings of political alienation?"[95] Elsewhere, Long writes, "The political reality model assumes that the individual is capable of accurately perceiving the dynamics of the sociopolitical system and, as a result, somehow reaches the affective state of political alienation."[96] Long concludes that "this explanation is fundamentally a variant of the S-R model, which does not stress the mediational processes linking the perceptual and affective domains. This model, therefore, lacks a motivational system which transforms the person's perceptions of systemic functioning into the person's feelings of systemic rejection."[97]

It should be recognized, however, that the political-reality explanation does not depend upon children correctly perceiving political realities. In the first place, even if black children do not understand political realities, they may learn feelings of political powerlessness and distrust from black adults who do. Second, the political-reality explanation is not based merely upon a theoretical distinction between perceptions and feelings, but upon the assumption that blacks have less political power than whites and that political leaders are less trustworthy in their dealings with blacks than in their dealings with whites. And, while we welcome attempts to elaborate more fully the linkages involved in the explanation, we would agree with Sears that no complex formulations are likely to be useful given our present state of knowledge about the political socialization process.

Last, we may mention Bruce A. Campbell's test.[98] As we saw in Chapter 4, Campbell attempted to explain racial differences in anti-administration attitudes toward Watergate.[99] Drawing upon Orum and Cohen, upon my earlier formulation, and upon Rodgers, he speculated that the "political reality experienced by blacks encourages cynicism toward government, and therefore tends to be accompanied by a negative evaluation of Watergate."[100] Campbell did not discuss the political realities actually faced by blacks, however, but relied upon a measure of perceived racial discrimination.[101] He found that for both blacks and whites, students who believed there was racial discrimination were more likely to have an anti-administration view, but, although relationships were in the predicted direction, they were weak. Campbell concluded that "even the political reality explanation which earlier research has found to be a valuable explanatory factor failed to generate strong relationships in our data."[102]

Campbell's test of perceptions of political reality was weak, for he focused on racial discrimination and measured neither knowledge of nor beliefs about actual political power arrangements. But even if he had developed a better measure of perceptions of reality, his test would have been questionable, because, as we earlier argued, the explanations we developed attempt to account for racial differences in more generalized feelings of political efficacy and trust, not reactions to a specific political event.[103]

EVALUATION OF THE POLITICAL-REALITY EXPLANATION

The political-reality explanation has one main weakness. We were unable to explain the processes through which children learn about political realities and the way this knowledge may contribute to low feelings of political efficacy and trust. On the other hand, the explanation has considerable strength. It can account for both basic findings and, moreover, it is parsimonious. And, even though we cannot easily measure political power, few would deny that blacks are deprived of political power and have fewer sanctions over political leaders. The political-reality explanation also leads to a series of additional empirical consequences that were supported by extant socialization research.

In our review of discussions and tests of the explanations, we also found that Sears, Morris, Rodgers, and Long all favored the political-reality explanation. Sears concluded that explanations based upon simple social-learning theory, such as the political-reality explanation, were both more parsimonious and powerful than complex social-psychological explanations. Morris preferred a subcultural explanation, but he favored the political-reality explanation over the social-deprivation explanation. Whereas the relationships postulated by the social-deprivation explanation were not always supported by available data, the assumptions of the political-reality explanation seemed highly plausible. Rodgers found little support for the social-deprivation explanation, although he concluded it warranted further testing, but he argued that there was considerable support for the political-reality explanation. Long concluded that the political-reality explanation had considerably more explanatory power than the social-deprivation explanation. Among scholars who have attempted to test the political-reality explanation, only Campbell failed to find support for it, and he relied upon a dependent variable of questionable validity.

It seems to us, however, that the political-reality explanation gains its greatest plausibility by being the only explanation that can begin to account for the time-series differences in political trust. Between 1954, with the Supreme Court school desegregation decision, and 1965, with the Voting Rights Act of that year, blacks made consistent gains at the national level, and this may have contributed to high trust toward national-level officials. But blacks scored few political gains at the national level after 1965, for the escalating Vietnam war forced Johnson to defer his Great Society reforms.[104] By the summer of 1967, when black schoolchildren began to manifest low levels of political trust, widespread riots were devastating major American cities. Although it would be difficult to demonstrate that political leaders were less trustworthy toward blacks after the spring of 1967, black perceptions of their trustworthiness clearly seemed to have changed. This decline in trust may not stem from any actual lowered "trustworthiness" among political leaders, but may have been affected by the reality of decreasing black political effectiveness at the national level.[105]

But this interpretation raises a problem, for there have been no marked changes in racial differences in feelings of political effectiveness. Admittedly, as the data in Table 6–1 demonstrate, racial differences among adults were somewhat greater in 1974 than they had been a decade earlier, but the overall trend shows considerable continuity. Moreover, the data for preadults, summarized in Appendix A, show no marked increases in racial differences, and the most representative data on efficacy among preadults, the two SRC surveys reported by M. Kent Jennings, suggest that racial differences may have diminished. The political-reality explanation, some may argue, should predict increasing racial differences in feelings of political effectiveness. We will attempt to resolve this anomaly when we comparatively evaluate the explanations in the following chapter.[106]

NOTES

1. For an early article that was sensitive to the effects of political realities on feelings of political efficacy and trust, see Edgar Litt, "Political Cynicism and Political Futility," *Journal of Politics,* 25 (May 1963), pp. 312–323. For a more recent study that specifically focuses on feelings of efficacy among blacks, see William H. Form and Joan Huber, "Income, Race, and the Ideology of Political Efficacy," *Journal of Politics,* 33 (August 1971), pp. 659–688.

Because of the decline in trust in recent years, political scientists have become increasingly sensitized to this possibility. See Philip E. Converse, "Change in the American Electorate," in *The Human Meaning of Social Change,* eds. Angus Campbell and Philip E. Converse (New York: Russell Sage, 1972), pp. 263–337, at pp. 324–337; Arthur H. Miller, "Political Issues and Trust in Government, 1964–1970," *American Political Science Review,* 68 (September 1974), pp. 951–972; Jack Citrin, "Comment: The Political Relevance of Trust in Government," *American Political Science Review,* 68 (September 1974), pp. 973–988; Citrin, *Political Disaffection in America* (Englewood Cliffs, N.J.: Prentice-Hall, forthcoming): and James D. Wright, *The Dissent of the Governed: Alienation and Democracy in America* (New York: Academic Press, 1976).

For an interesting study that claims to find no support for the political-reality thesis among American adults, see Robert Weissberg, "Political Efficacy and Political Illusion," *Journal of Politics,* 37 (May 1975), pp. 469–487. However, Weissberg's test used rather indirect measures of the respondent's actual political power, such as whether he lived in a congressional district represented by his own party and whether he lived in a competitive congressional district. Such factors are clearly not as important as the profound political differences that divide black and white Americans.

2. See Joan E. Laurence, "White Socialization: Black Reality," *Psychiatry,* 33 (May 1970), pp. 174–194, and Edward S. Greenberg, "Children and Government: A Comparison Across Racial Lines," *Midwest Journal of Political*

Science, 14 (May 1970), pp. 249–275. Jewel L. Prestage makes a similar argument, maintaining that blacks form a separate political subculture. See "Black Politics and the Kerner Report: Concerns and Directions," in *Blacks in the United States,* eds. Norval D. Glenn and Charles M. Bonjean (San Francisco: Chandler, 1969), pp. 538–549.

3. For example, see Harrell R. Rodgers, Jr., "Toward Explanation of the Political Efficacy and Political Cynicism of Black Adolescents: An Exploratory Study," *American Journal of Political Science,* 18 (May 1974), pp. 257–282; Thomas J. Williams, "Subcultural Differences in Political Socialization among Selected Children in Georgia," unpublished Ph.D. dissertation, University of Georgia, 1972; Williams, "Racial Differences in Southern Children's Attitudes Toward Presidential Authority," *Georgia Political Science Association Journal,* 2 (Spring 1974), pp. 89–121; Harold M. Barger, "Images of the President and Policemen among Black, Mexican-American and Anglo School Children: Considerations on Watergate," paper presented at 70th Annual Meeting of American Political Science Association, August-September 1974; and several papers by Samuel Long, especially, "Political Alienation among Black and White Adolescents: A Test of the Social Deprivation and Political Reality Models," *American Politics Quarterly,* 4 (July 1976), pp. 267–303.

4. Robert A. Dahl, *A Preface to Democratic Theory* (Chicago: University of Chicago Press, 1956), pp. 116–118.

5. See Louis L. Knowles and Kenneth Prewitt, eds., *Institutional Racism in America* (Englewood Cliffs, N.J.: Prentice-Hall, 1969), pp. 91–93. However, some black congressmen are now beginning to build considerable seniority, although at the very time that congressional reforms are weakening the seniority system. As Lucius J. Barker and Jesse J. McCorry, Jr., write, "It would indeed be ironic if the influence of seniority diminishes about the very time that blacks gain in seniority." See *Black Americans and the Political System* (Cambridge, Mass.: Winthrop, 1976), p. 283.

6. See Nelson W. Polsby and Aaron B. Wildavsky, *Presidential Elections: Strategies of American Electoral Politics,* 4th ed. (New York: Scribner's, 1976), pp. 171–172.

7. Five separate studies have found black children to be less politically knowledgeable than white children were. See Kenneth P. Langton and M. Kent Jennings, "Political Socialization and the High School Civics Curriculum in the United States," *American Political Science Review,* 62 (September 1968), pp. 852–867, at pp. 859–860; Henry I. Penfield, "The Political Socialization of the Alabama School Child," unpublished Ph.D. dissertation, University of Alabama, 1970, pp. 63–68; Joan E. Laurence, "White Socialization: Black Reality," p. 178; Edward S. Greenberg, "Political Socialization to Support of the System: A Comparison of Black and White Children," unpublished Ph.D. dissertation, University of Wisconsin, 1969, pp. 84–100; Thomas J. Williams, "Subcultural Differences," p. 70–71. On the other hand, Anthony M. Orum and Roberta S. Cohen found that at some grade levels black children were more politically knowledgeable than white children were. See "The Development of Political Orientations among Black and White Children," *American Sociological Review,* 38 (February 1973), pp. 62–74, at pp. 67–68.

8. See Arthur Kornhauser, Harold L. Sheppard, and Albert J. Mayer, *When Labor Votes: A Study of Auto Workers* (New York: University Books, 1956), p. 157; and Sheldon S. Stryker, "The Urban Scene: Observations from Research," *The Review* (Indiana University), 11 (Summer 1969), pp. 8–17.

9. The original sense of political efficacy scale had five items, but one was dropped after 1952. Although the SRC later added new efficacy items, I restrict my presentation to those that have been used from 1952 on. Moreover, the items in Table 6–1 are highly comparable to those used to measure feelings of political efficacy among schoolchildren, for socialization researchers have adapted the SRC items for research among preadults. The newer efficacy items have not been used among schoolchildren.

10. The data upon which tables 6–1 and 6–2 were based were provided by the Inter-University Consortium for Political Research, which bears no responsibility for my analyses or interpretations. I am grateful to Thomas O. Jukam for his assistance in creating the data files from which these analyses were conducted, and especially for his assistance with the analysis for Table 6–2.

11. As Herbert H. Hyman demonstrates, the rise in efficacy among blacks was concentrated in the South. See his "Dimensions of Socio-Psychological Change in the Negro Population," in *The Human Meaning of Social Change*, eds. Angus Campbell and Philip E. Converse (New York: Russell Sage, 1972), pp. 339–390, at pp. 371–373.

12. Philip E. Converse argues that the rising proportion who see ways other than voting as a method of influencing the government resulted from the increased use of nonconventional participation, especially by the civil rights movement and by opponents of the Vietnam war. His analysis (conducted through 1968) demonstrates that the greatest increases in efficacy on this item were among white college graduates. See his "Change in the American Electorate," pp. 327–329.

13. M. Kent Jennings and Richard G. Niemi, "The Transmission of Political Values from Parent to Child," *American Political Science Review*, 62 (March 1968), pp. 169–184; Jack Dennis, *Political Learning in Childhood and Adolescence: A Study of Fifth, Eighth, and Eleventh Graders in Milwaukee, Wisconsin* (Madison: Wisconsin Research and Development Center for Cognitive Learning, 1969), pp. 46–48; and Robert E. Dowse and John Hughes, "The Family, the School and the Political Socialization Process, *Sociology*, 5 (January 1971), pp. 21–45.

For a conflicting view that argues that the low correlations between parent-child political attitudes may result partly from measurement problems, see Robert Weissberg and Richard Joslyn, "Methodological Appropriateness in Political Socialization Research," in *Handbook of Political Socialization: Theory and Research*, ed. Stanley Allen Renshon (New York: Free Press, forthcoming).

14. Dennis, *Political Learning*, pp. 46–48.

15. Based upon a personal communication. The basic conclusions reached by Jennings and Niemi concerning the failure of children to learn their parents' political values applied to both black and white students.

16. See Prestage, "Black Politics." For a more extensive discussion of the subcultural socialization thesis, see Orum and Cohen, "The Development of Political Orientations," pp. 70–71. For a critique of the subcultural socialization thesis, see pp. 90–91.

17. Harrell R. Rodgers, Jr., and George Taylor, "The Policeman as an Agent of Regime Legitimation," *Midwest Journal of Political Science*, 15 (February 1971), pp. 72–86, at pp. 82–86.

18. David O. Sears and John B. McConahay, *The Politics of Violence: The New Urban Blacks and the Watts Riot* (Boston: Houghton Mifflin, 1973), p. 191.

19. The precise item was: "Some people say that whites and Negroes are treated the same. Do you think this statement is... true... false... I don't know."

Although the Greenberg item does not specifically refer to treatment by the government, it was asked within the overall context of a politically oriented questionnaire. Earlier in the questionnaire, for example, children were asked whether "all people should be treated the same by the government."

20. Greenberg, "Political Socialization to Support of the System," p. 297.

21. *Ibid.,* p. 303.

22. Rodgers, "Toward Explanation," pp. 275–276. This index is described on pp. 91–92.

23. Rodgers, "Toward Explanation of the Political Efficacy and Political Cynicism of Black Schoolchildren," paper presented at Annual Meeting of Southwestern Social Science Association, San Antonio, March-April 1972, p. 19. These relationships were not reported in the published version of Rodgers' paper. All other citations of "Toward Explanation" refer to Rodgers' article in the May 1974 *American Journal of Political Science*.

24. Rodgers, "Toward Explanation," p. 276.

25. *Ibid.,* p. 277.

26. *Ibid.*

27. Long, "Political Alienation," p. 297.

28. These measures are described more fully on p. 105.

29. *Ibid.,* p. 296. See Appendix C for a description of these measures.

30. *Ibid.,* pp. 287–288.

31. *Ibid.,* p. 288.

32. See pp. 91–96.

33. James T. Jones, "Political Socialization in a Mid-Western Industrial Community," unpublished Ph.D. dissertation, University of Illinois, 1965, p. 166.

34. Rodgers, "Toward Explanation," p. 265.

35. Johnson received about one in seven of his votes from blacks, and both Humphrey and McGovern received about one in five of their votes from blacks. See Robert Axelrod, "Where the Votes Come From: An Analysis of Electoral Coalitions, 1952–1968," *American Political Science Review,* 68 (March 1972), pp. 11–20; Axelrod, "Communication," *American Political Science Review,* 68

(June 1974), pp. 717–720; and Paul R. Abramson, *Generational Change in American Politics* (Lexington, Mass.: Heath, 1975), pp. 23–26.

36. Roberta S. Sigel, "An Exploration into Some Aspects of Political Socialization: Some Children's Reactions to the Death of a President," in *Children and the Death of a President: Multi-disciplinary Studies,* eds. Martha Wolfenstein and Gilbert Kliman (Garden City, N.Y.: Doubleday, Anchor Books, 1965), pp. 36–69, at pp. 58–59. A National Opinion Research Center study of adults conducted shortly after President Kennedy's assassination showed that blacks were more personally upset and concerned than white respondents were. See Paul B. Sheatsley and Jacob J. Feldman, "The Assassination of President Kennedy: A Preliminary Report on Public Reactions and Behavior," *Public Opinion Quarterly,* 28 (Summer 1964), pp. 189–215, at pp. 197–200.

37. Dean Jaros, "Children's Orientations Toward Political Authority: A Detroit Study," unpublished Ph.D. dissertation, Vanderbilt University, 1966, p. 101; and Jaros, "Children's Orientations Toward the President: Some Additional Theoretical Considerations and Data," *Journal of Politics,* 29 (May 1967), pp. 368–387, at p. 381.

38. Penfield, "The Political Socialization of the Alabama School Child," p. 94.

39. Greenberg, "Black Children and the Political System," *Public Opinion Quarterly,* 34 (Fall 1970), pp. 334–345, at pp. 340–341.

40. Merton S. Krause, "Schoolchildren's Attitudes Toward Public Authority Figures," Chicago, Institute for Juvenile Research, August 1972, mimeo, pp. 7–9. See Appendix A for a more detailed report.

41. Alden J. Stevens, "Children's Acquisition of Regime Norms in Subcultures of Race and Social Class: The Problem of System Maintenance," unpublished Ph.D. dissertation, University of Maryland, 1969, p. 83.

42. Williams, "Racial Differences," p. 111.

43. *Ibid.,* p. 120. Williams was referring to my formulation in the November 1972 *Journal of Politics*.

44. Pauline Marie Vaillancourt, "The Political Socialization of Young People: A Panel Survey of Youngsters in the San Francisco Bay Area," unpublished Ph.D. dissertation, University of California at Berkeley, 1972, pp. 70–72. See Appendix A for the actual presidential trust scores.

45. *Ibid.*

46. David O. Sears, "Political Socialization," in *Handbook of Political Science, Volume 2: Micropolitical Theory,* eds. Fred I. Greenstein and Nelson W. Polsby (Reading, Mass.: Addison-Wesley, 1975), pp. 93–153, at p. 109.

47. Orum and Cohen, "The Development of Political Orientations," p. 67. This persistent tendency for blacks to be less supportive of the president than whites also held in a subsequent analysis in which controls for sex were also introduced. See Anthony M. Orum, Roberta S. Cohen, Sherri Grasmuck, and Amy W. Orum, "Sex, Socialization and Politics," *American Sociological Review,* 39 (April 1974), pp. 197–209, at p. 201.

48. Barger, "Images of the President," p. 12. See Appendix A for a more detailed report.

49. *Ibid.*, pp. 14–15. However, there were negligible differences on the view that the president would help the child's family. See Barger, "Images of the President," p. 21.

50. *Ibid.*, pp. 12–15.

51. Based upon a personal communication. See Appendix A for a more detailed report.

52. Dean Jaros and Kenneth L. Kolson, "The Multifarious Leader: Political Socialization of Amish, 'Yanks,' Blacks," in *The Politics of Future Citizens: New Dimensions in the Political Socialization of Children,* ed. Richard G. Niemi (San Francisco: Jossey-Bass, 1974), pp. 41–62, at p. 54. See Appendix A for a more detailed report.

53. *Ibid.*, pp. 45–46.

54. Based upon a personal communication. See Appendix A for a more detailed report.

55. See especially his discussion in Richard C. Remy and James A. Nathan, "The Future of Political Systems: What Young People Think," *Futures,* 6 (December 1974), pp. 463–476, at pp. 465–466.

56. Fred I. Greenstein, "The Benevolent Leader Revisited: Children's Images of Political Leaders in Three Democracies," *American Political Science Review,* 69 (December 1975), pp. 1371–1398, at p. 1384.

57. *Ibid.*, p. 1396.

58. David O. Sears, *Political Attitudes Through the Life Cycle* (San Francisco: Freeman, forthcoming). As Sears' book is still in press, pagination cannot be provided. Quotations from Sears' book may be altered somewhat in his final version.

59. Milton D. Morris, *The Politics of Black Americans* (New York: Harper and Row, 1975), p. 143.

60. *Ibid.*

61. *Ibid.*, p. 144.

62. Orum and Cohen, "The Development of Political Orientations," p. 70.

63. *Ibid.*

64. See p. 79.

65. Their measure, which was used only with children in the seventh through the twelfth grades, was based on the following seven items:

"For the black, equality and integration are not the same thing."

"It is up to the government to make sure that everyone has a secure job and a good standard of living."

"If black people are not getting fair treatment in jobs and housing, the government should see to it that they do."

"The 'Afro' or 'natural' hairstyle is dignified."

"Black officials have a duty to be honest and should be more protective of the black community."

"The government in Washington should see to it that white and black children go to the same schools."

"Many police departments are trying to wipe out militant black organizations and their leaders."

66. Orum and Cohen, The Development of Political Orientations," pp. 71–72.

67. My *Journal of Politics* article and the Orum and Cohen article appeared within a few months of each other, and we had no opportunity to review each other's work before our respective articles appeared.

68. Morris, *The Politics of Black Americans,* pp. 144–145.

69. Rodgers, "Toward Explanation," p. 275.

70. *Ibid.,* pp. 275–276.

71. *Ibid.,* p. 276.

72. See pp. 84–85.

73. Rodgers, Toward Explanation," p. 277.

74. As Rodgers correctly reports, Langton and Jennings found that among Southern blacks seniors who had taken a civics course were somewhat more politically cynical than those who had not. But they found, contrary to Rodgers, that Southern blacks who had taken a civics course felt more politically efficacious than those who had not. Such differences could result from differences in the samples, differences in the time period when these samples were conducted, or, given the small Ns that obtain when so many controls are introduced, from sampling error. For their discussion of the effects of the civics curriculum on Southern blacks, see Langton and Jennings, "Political Socialization and the High School Civics Curriculum," p. 865.

75. Kenneth P. Langton and David A. Karns, "The Relative Influence of the Family, Peer Group, and School in the Development of Political Efficacy," *Western Political Quarterly,* 21 (December 1969), pp. 813–826, at p. 815.

76. The reliability of this information may be questioned, however, for children are not good informants about levels of political interest within the home. (See Richard G. Niemi, *How Family Members Perceive Each Other: Political and Social Attitudes in Two Generations* [New Haven, Conn.: Yale University Press, 1974], pp. 63–65.) But Niemi did not directly measure the accuracy of students' reports of political discussion within the home. Moreover, Rodgers' data measure the extent to which children say they discuss politics, and may be more reliable than reports about the political behavior of parents.

77. Rodgers, "Toward Explanation," p. 277.

78. *Ibid.,* p. 278.

79. *Ibid.*

80. *Ibid.,* pp. 279–80.

81. *Ibid.,* p. 279.

82. Long, "Political Alienation." Long presented two earlier tests of the political-reality explanation with his St. Louis data. See, "Sociopolitical Reality and Political Alienation: A Comparison of White and Black Adolescents," paper presented at 29th Annual Meeting of Western Political Science Associa-

tion, Seattle, March, 1975, and "Sociopolitical Antecedents of Political Alienation among Black and White Adolescents: Social Deprivation and/or Political Reality?," paper presented at 70th Annual Meeting of American Sociological Association, San Francisco, August, 1975. These earlier versions will be cited only where they contain information omitted from the published version of Long's test.

83. Long also developed measures of perceived racial discrimination, perceived economic discrimination, and perceived system blame, but they do not measure perceptions of political reality. See Long, "Political Alienation," p. 297.

84. The following items were used to measure "perceived black political inefficacy":

"Black people don't have much say in how our government is run."

"Black citizens have more political power than white citizens." (Reflected so that disagreement is scored as perceived black political ineffectiveness.)

"Our political leaders don't really care about the needs of black people."

"White people have more influence in our government than black people do."

"A black man has a much better chance of influencing our political leaders than does a white man." (Reflected so that disagreement is scored as perceived black political ineffectiveness.)

85. The following items were used to measure "perceived black political distrust":

"Most politicians really don't represent the interests of black people."

"White citizens have more reason to trust our political leaders than black citizens do."

"Our political leaders seem more interested in helping black people than in helping white people." (Reflected so that disagreement is scored as perceived black political distrust.)

"Politicians give black people what they want more often than they give white people what they want." (Reflected so that disagreement is scored as perceived black political distrust.)

"Black people have no reason to believe what politicians tell them."

86. Long, "Political Alienation," pp. 286–287. However, these data are presented in greater detail in "Sociopolitical Reality," pp. 9–11. In the earlier paper, Long reports the mean scores by race for each item.

87. Long, "Political Alienation," pp. 287–288. As we noted above, in our view Long's political estrangement scale measures neither feelings of political efficacy nor of political trust. See p. 51.

88. However, Long's test is weak for he employed a combined measure of perceptions of political reality that included perceived racial discrimination, perceived economic discrimination, and perceived system blame. See "Political Alienation," pp. 296–297. Moreover, his combined alienation measure included his political estrangement scale, and his self-confidence scale included measures of both self-esteem and locus of control. Using these gross measures could easily conceal important relationships that might emerge if more refined controls were employed.

89. Long, "Political Alienation," pp. 289–290.

90. *Ibid.*, p. 289.

91. Long, "Sociopolitical Reality," pp. 18–20.

92. Long also presented a canonical correlation analysis in which he examined results separately for whites and for blacks. See "Sociopolitical Reality," pp. 15–17. He did not explain why his principal component analysis was conducted for the combined sample of blacks and whites.

93. Long, "Political Alienation," p. 291.

94. *Ibid.* Here Long cites Albert Ellis, *Reason and Emotion in Psychotherapy* (New York: Lyle Stuart, 1962).

95. Long, "Political Alienation," p. 292.

96. Long, "Cognitive-Perceptual Factors in the Political Alienation Process: A Test of Six Models," paper presented at 34th Annual Meeting of Midwest Political Science Association, Chicago, April-May 1976, p. 3. Also see, Long, "Political Disenchantment: A Cognitive Perceptual Theory of Political Alienation," paper presented at Annual Meeting of Southwestern Politicial Science Association, Dallas, April 1976. Although both of these papers present tests of the political-reality explanation, and although Long's "Cognitive-Perceptual Factors" paper claims to support it, we have not discussed these papers here, for they do not focus on the political attitudes of black preadults.

97. Long, "Cognitive-Perceptual Factors," p. 3.

98. See Bruce A. Campbell, "Racial Differences in the Reaction to Watergate: Some Implications for Political Support," *Youth and Society,* 7 (June 1976), pp. 439–460.

99. See pp. 53–54 above.

100. Campbell, "Racial Differences," p. 449.

101. The following items were used to measure perceptions of discrimination:

"Do you think that in Georgia, many, some or few blacks miss out on good housing because white owners will not rent or sell to them?"

"Do you think that in Georgia, many, some, or few blacks miss out on jobs and promotions because of racial discrimination?"

"On the average, blacks in Georgia have worse jobs, education, and housing than white people. Do you think this is due mainly to blacks being discriminated against, or mainly due to something about Negroes themselves?"

102. Campbell, "Racial Differences," p. 451.

103. See p. 53 above.

104. See Daniel P. Moynihan, *Maximum Feasible Misunderstanding: Community Action in the War on Poverty* (New York: Free Press, 1969).

105. In his critique of the political-reality explanation, Ted Tapper correctly notes that after 1964 "at the local level the number of Afro-Americans moving into positions of real power expanded." (See Ted Tapper, *Political Education and Stability: Elite Responses to Political Conflict* [New York: Wiley, 1976], p. 164). "I mention this," Tapper adds, "because Abramson argues that if political leaders were elected by black votes (as was undoubtedly true of the

black mayors who emerged in the 1960s) this would increase levels of political trust." (*Political Education,* p. 183.) While Tapper is correct, most studies of political efficacy and trust focus on national-level authorities. There have not yet been adequate studies to determine whether electing black officials increases local feelings of efficacy and trust.

106. See pp. 110–111.

Chapter 7. Comparative Evaluation of the Explanations

Of the four explanations I advanced, only the intelligence explanation can be rejected, for there is little reason why intelligence, as a set of cognitive abilities, should contribute to feelings of political effectiveness, and still less why it should contribute to political trust. And, even if high intelligence contributes to feelings of political effectiveness among whites, it may have the reverse effect among blacks, for more intelligent blacks may be more cognizant of the political powerlessness of black Americans. Moreover, the only two studies that tested the relationship between measured intelligence and feelings of political efficacy among black schoolchildren yielded contradictory results. While the intelligence explanation can be tested easily by socialization researchers who have access to intelligence scores, it seems unlikely that racial differences in intelligence account for the weak feelings of political effectiveness among black Americans. Also, we found little theoretical reason that intelligence should contribute to feelings of political trust.

The political-education explanation may explain weak feelings of political effectiveness among black schoolchildren, but because it is essentially silent about feelings of trust it has less scope than either the social-deprivation or political-reality explanations. Moreover, the political-education explanation rests on the questionable assumption that schools are effective agents of political socialization. We have scant data to support this assumption, although research about the actual content of political education, as well as the effect of school climates, is certainly warranted. Still, it should be remembered that children learn about politics from many sources other than schools, and that the impact of the school as a socialization agent is therefore weakened. In addition, the political-education explanation has a major logical limitation; it cannot account for the low political trust among black schoolchildren.

The social-deprivation explanation has considerable scope for it can explain both findings. The assumptions on which it rests can be supported theoretically, and there is empirical evidence that these assumptions are true. But although the bulk of the available data supports each of its five assumptions, in some cases Assumptions B.2, B.3, and B.5 were not supported by available data. Even where the assumptions were supported, the relationships between social deprivation and self-confidence, while certainly respectable given the problems inherent in survey research, were not particularly strong. Even if we had highly reliable and valid measures of social deprivation, deprivation probably could not explain very much of the variation in feelings of self-confidence. Moreover, the relationships between feelings of self-confidence and feelings of political efficacy and trust were often weak. Thus, even reliable and valid measures of self-confidence would probably not explain very much of the variation in feelings of political efficacy and trust. So it seems highly unlikely that the social-deprivation explanation by itself accounts for all the racial variation in feelings of political efficacy and trust. Admittedly, we have no direct data as to whether controlling for social deprivation and self-confidence would eliminate racial differences in feelings of efficacy and trust, but it seems unlikely that such controls would do more than reduce racial differences in these attitudes. Even so, the social-deprivation explanation may be a valid partial explanation for racial differences. However, the explanation has one major limitation: it cannot explain the relative decline in black political trust that occurred during and after the summer of 1967.

The political-reality explanation has considerable scope and is also the most parsimonious. But it rests on the assumption that black children learn about political realities, or are indirectly influenced by black adults who do know these realities. How such attitudes are conveyed is difficult to explain convincingly, especially in view of the evidence that attitudes such as political efficacy and political cynicism are seldom transmitted from parent to child. The concept of political "subculture" may help to explain how feelings of political powerlessness and cynicism are learned, but the subcultural socialization formulation needs to be developed more fully and tested more directly if we are to understand how subcultural norms are communicated.[1] Even though we know little about the processes through which political realities are learned, or the way knowledge about these realities affects feelings of political powerlessness and cynicism, the political-reality explanation did lead to several additional empirical consequences that were supported by extant socialization research. Moreover, even though the tests of this explanation by Harrell R. Rodgers, Jr., and by Samuel Long were weaker than they claimed, it would be foolish to ignore their basic conclusion: the political-reality explanation received far more support than the social-deprivation explanation.[2]

The political-reality explanation gains its greatest plausibility by providing an explanation for the decline in black political trust during and after the summer of 1967. Between 1954 and 1965 blacks made consistent gains at the national level. But they made few gains after the Voting Rights Act of 1965, and by the summer of 1967, when blacks first began to manifest low political trust, widespread riots erupted in major American cities. Perhaps political leaders had not become less trustworthy toward blacks, but black perceptions of their trustworthiness may have been affected by the reality of decreasing black effectiveness at the national political level. But this interpretation raises a problem, for racial differences in feelings of political effectiveness did not grow after the summer of 1967. Although no clear time-series trend can be established, the Michigan SRC sample of high school seniors found that racial differences in feelings of political effectiveness had decreased. Can we account for this anomaly?

A closer look at the two Michigan surveys reported by M. Kent Jennings (see Appendix A) shows that between 1965 and 1973 feelings of political effectiveness dropped among blacks on all three of the efficacy items used in both of these years. This would be consistent with our argument that blacks lost political power during this period. But feelings of political effectiveness dropped far more among whites, and racial differences were eliminated on two of these items. In part, the drop in feelings of efficacy among blacks may have been checked by a statistical "floor" effect: these feelings were already quite low in 1965, and they simply had less room to fall. But it is also possible that increased feelings of black pride and self-confidence slowed down the decline in feelings of political effectiveness.

Throughout our analysis, we have found that feelings of self-confidence were more consistently correlated with feelings of political effectiveness than with feelings of political trust. This makes sense theoretically, for if a person feels he can control his social environment he may also feel he can control his political environment, whereas feelings of self-confidence contribute to feelings of political trust through a more indirect process. Although we lack adequate time-series data about feelings of self-confidence, it is plausible that some dimensions of self-confidence, especially feelings of self-worth, may have increased as a result of assertions of racial pride. This increased self-confidence may have slowed down the decline in political effectiveness among blacks, but failed to prevent a rapid decline in political trust. If so, the social-deprivation explanation may be a better tool for explaining racial differences in feelings of political effectiveness than it is for explaining feelings of political trust. But the political-reality explanation may be more useful in accounting for racial differences in feelings of political trust than it is in explaining feelings of political effectiveness, for the latter may be more strongly influenced by psychological attributes.

In any event, the social-deprivation and the political-reality explanations are not mutually exclusive, for both could contribute to some of the racial variation in feelings of political effectiveness and political trust. It may be difficult to evaluate their relative explanatory power, for social deprivation and political powerlessness tend to covary: where blacks have social opportunities they are more likely to have political power, and where blacks have political power they can use it to increase their social opportunities. And, while these two explanations may lead to different empirical consequences, these consequences will not be contradictory.

We might be able to develop a higher level explanation that incorporates both the social-deprivation and the political-reality explanations. For example, a "deprivation" explanation could be devised that included both social and political deprivation. But this would probably serve little useful purpose for a higher level explanation would probably not lead us to generate propositions not already advanced by the two lower level explanations.

THEORETICAL AND RESEARCH IMPLICATIONS

The explanations developed in this book are simple. The assumptions constituting these explanations can all, in principle at least, be tested empirically—although Assumptions D.1 and D.2 go well beyond the scope of political-socialization research. The empirical consequences that I derived from these explanations are also testable. But because socialization research has been so largely atheoretical, I was seldom able to test these assumptions or consequences. Although political socialization researchers have been guided by theories about what attitudes contribute to the maintenance of democratic politics, they have seldom either developed or tested hypotheses about the conditions that contribute to attitudinal variation. It is difficult to develop grounded theory out of atheoretical research. Nonetheless, a careful evaluation of the assumptions that constitute the four basic explanations should provide some theoretical guidance for future students of the political socialization process.

In the first place, we must recognize that subcultural variation may be an important source of attitudinal differences. Early socialization studies often focused on modal socialization patterns, even though most modern societies have a wide range of social class, ethnic, racial, or religious diversity, and this diversity may contribute to different political attitudes among subgroups. Unlike students of modal socialization patterns, who may consciously avoid studying structural arrangements, students of subcultural socialization must attempt to specify social *and* political structures that contribute to differential learning among social groups.

But although this study attempts to explain attitudinal differences between blacks and whites, its theoretical implications go beyond analyzing racial differences. The explanations advanced here could be used to account for variation in feelings of political efficacy and trust among whites and, in some cases, they could explain the absence of racial differences. Where whites are deprived of opportunity and respect, they may feel less efficacious and trusting than blacks. Moreover, some political events may be more likely to erode feelings of efficacy and trust among whites than among blacks, in which case the political-reality explanation suggests that whites might develop weaker feelings of political efficacy and trust than blacks.

This analysis also forces us to recognize that political socialization is an ongoing process. David O. Sears lamented that the few results we now have about the political-socialization process may easily be time bound.[3] Sears is certainly correct, but changing relationships over time have important theoretical implications. Our review of extant socialization research suggests not only that political attitudes change—witness the decline in political trust among the boys in Bachman's panel study—but that attitudes may change differentially for different social groups. It is not enough to recognize that political attitudes change. Political-socialization researchers have often given lip service to this fact. Theorists about the political-socialization process must (a) specify which political attitudes are more likely to change than other attitudes; (b) explain why some political attitudes are more likely to change than other attitudes; and (c) specify the conditions under which given attitudes are likely to change.

What we may need is an attempt to specify which political attitudes are strongly affected by personality characteristics and which are more likely to be affected by political conditions. Our preliminary assessment, based upon our review of extant socialization findings as well as a consideration of the theoretical linkages involved, is that feelings of personal effectiveness may be more strongly related to feelings of political effectiveness than they are to feelings of political trust. But both feelings of political effectiveness and of political trust can be affected by the specific political setting in which political socialization—and resocialization—occurs.

The research implications of this book are fairly extensive. By demonstrating that there is already considerable support for certain findings, this study suggests that mere replication will have little theoretical pay off. At least some students of subcultural political socialization have gone beyond merely reporting differences to advance explanations for their findings. What we may need, however, are research designs that allow us to test between explanations.

My earlier formulation of these explanations has already led to such designs and this book will, we hope, stimulate further research. By carefully spelling out the assumptions underlying the basic explanations, we have pointed directly to hypotheses that need testing through future empirical research. Several research problems seem crucial. We need to know what is being taught in the schools and could use additional information about differing school climates. Such data can probably best be obtained through open-ended strategies relying on participant observation and through using students as informants as well as mere respondents. To examine the social-deprivation explanation, political scientists must not only measure social deprivation, but must study the role of self-confidence as an intervening psychological variable. More attention must be given to developing measures of self-confidence. Political scientists should also determine whether social deprivation directly affects feelings of political powerlessness and cynicism, without intervening social-psychological mechanisms.

The political-reality explanation, which seems so intuitively appealing, deserves serious research consideration. The plausibility of this explanation might be increased through quasi-experimental panel studies that examined political attitudes among black children before and after a political event that provided a direct test of the political power of blacks—for example, a mayoral election with a black candidate. Panel studies, as we have shown with the Bachman survey, may be particularly useful in testing the plausibility of the political-reality explanation. And even though mere replication of findings should not be the goal for individual researchers, there are sizable benefits to be gained from the continued use of similar items over time, for the resulting pool of time-series information may prove invaluable in assessing the political-reality explanation. Researchers should remember, however, that in the final analysis the political-reality explanation can best be supported by identifying the processes through which children learn to respond to the complex political environment in which they live.

NOTES

1. See Anthony M. Orum and Roberta S. Cohen, "The Development of Political Orientations among Black and White Adolescents," *American Sociological Review,* 38 (February 1973), pp. 62–74, at pp. 70–71.

2. See Harrell R. Rodgers, Jr., "Toward Explanation of the Political Efficacy and Political Cynicism of Black Adolescents: An Exploratory Study," *American Journal of Political Science,* 18 (May 1974), pp. 257–282, and Samuel Long, "Political Alienation among Black and White Adolescents: A Test of the Social Deprivation and Political Reality Models," *American Politics Quarterly,* 4 (July 1976), pp. 267–303.

Even Bruce A. Campbell, who relied upon attitudes toward Watergate as his dependent variable, found somewhat more support for the political-reality explanation than the social-deprivation explanation. See Bruce A. Campbell, "Racial Differences in the Reaction to Watergate: Some Implications for Political Support," *Youth and Society,* 7 (June 1976), pp. 439–459.

3. David O. Sears, "Review of Langton, *Political Socialization;* Dawson and Prewitt, *Political Socialization;* and Easton and Dennis, *Children in the Political System," Midwest Journal of Political Science,* 15 (February 1971), at pp. 154–160, at p. 160.

APPENDIX A

Basic Findings about Feelings of
Political Efficacy and Political Trust, by
Race (Listed by Date of Survey)

RESEARCH REPORTED[a]	DATE OF SURVEY	RESEARCH SITE	GRADES SAMPLED	SAMPLE SIZE
Jones (1965)	Fall 1963	Gary, Indiana	8–12	295 blacks; 427 whites
Jennings (personal communication)	Spring 1965	National sample (question-naires)	12	About 1940 blacks; About 18,550 whites

(continued)

̍EASURE OF SENSE OF POLITICAL EFFICACY[b]	FINDING ABOUT EFFICACY	MEASURE OF POLITICAL TRUST[b]	FINDING ABOUT TRUST
̍gle m	76% of blacks did not agree family had no say about local government; 72% of whites did not agree.		
ree ms	39% of blacks disagreed that voting is only way people have a say about what the government does; 66% of whites disagreed. 26% of blacks disagreed that government is too complicated to understand; 33% of whites disagreed. 76% of blacks disagreed that their family has no say about what the government does; 87% of whites disagreed.	Five items	84% of blacks said the government in Washington could be trusted to do the right thing just about all the time or most of the time; 92% of whites said the government could be trusted to do the right thing. 74% of blacks said not very many or hardly any people running the government are crooked; 73% of whites said not very many or hardly any are crooked. 75% of blacks said the government doesn't waste much or wastes only some tax money; 66% of whites said the government doesn't waste much or wastes only some money. 77% of blacks said that almost all the people running the government usually know what they are doing; 81% of whites said they usually know what they are doing. 79% of blacks said the government was run for the benefit of all; 78% of whites said the government was run for the benefit of all.

(continued)

RESEARCH REPORTED[a]	DATE OF SURVEY	RESEARCH SITE	GRADES SAMPLED	SAMPLE SIZE
Langton and Jennings (1968) Jennings and Niemi (1974) (plus personal communication)	Spring 1965	National sample (interviews)	12	186 "non-whites"; 1480 whites
Bachman (1970) (plus personal communication)	Fall 1966	National sample (panel survey)	10 (boys only)	191 blacks (weighted N); 1604 whites (weighted N)
Penfield (1970)	February-May 1967	Birmingham, Florence, Mobile, Mountain Brook, Hale County, Winston County, Alabama	6,8,10,12	810 blacks; 1261 whites

(continued)

Measure of Sense of Political Efficacy[b]	Finding about Efficacy	Measure of Political Trust[b]	Finding about Trust
...o-item ...le	59% of blacks scored medium or high; 79% of whites scored medium or high.	Six-item political cynicism scale	77% of blacks scored medium or low on political cynicism; 79% of whites scored medium or low.
		Three-item political trust scale	$\bar{X}$ score for blacks $=3.74$ $\bar{X}$ score for whites $=3.68$
...r ...s	39% of blacks disagreed that "voting is the only way people like my mother and father can have any say about how the government runs things"; 48% of whites disagreed.	Five-item national government cynicism scale	65% of blacks scored low on political cynicism; 36% of whites scored low.
	75% of blacks disagreed that "my family doesn't have any say about what the government does"; 77% of whites disagreed.	Five-item state government cynicism scale	30% of blacks scored low on political cynicism; 44% of whites scored low.
	71% of blacks said the government pays "a good deal" or "some" attention to what the people think; 71% of whites said the government pays "a good deal" or "some" attention.		
	29% of blacks disagreed that "sometimes politics and government seem so complicated that a person like me can't really understand what is happening today"; 24% of whites disagreed.		

(continued)

RESEARCH REPORTED[a]	DATE OF SURVEY	RESEARCH SITE	GRADES SAMPLED	SAMPLE SIZE
Ehman (1969, 1972) (plus personal communication)	March 1967	Pontiac, Michigan (panel survey)	10	41 blacks; 62 whites
Kenyon (1969; 1970)	Spring 1967	Brooklyn, New York	8,10,12	98 blacks; about 780 whites
Dennis (1969)	Summer 1967	Milwaukee, Wisconsin	5,8,11	113 blacks; 147 whites
Masson (1971) (plus personal communication)	October 1967–May 1968	Seattle public schools	Ages 5 through 16	71 blacks; 139 whites
Laurence (1970)	March 1968	Sacramento, California	5,6,8	178 blacks; 821 whites

(continued)

Measure of Sense of Political Efficacy[b]	Finding about Efficacy	Measure of Political Trust[b]	Finding about Trust
...ur-item ...itical ...cacy ...le	X̄ score for blacks = 2.62 X̄ score for whites = 3.00	Four-item political cynicism scale	X̄ trust score for blacks = 3.17 X̄ trust score for whites = 3.65
...ee- ...n ...ex	53% of blacks felt politically efficacious; 61% of whites felt efficacious.	Seven-item political cynicism scale	29% of blacks scored low on political cynicism; 31% of whites scored low.
...ur-item ...ernment ...ponsive- ...s index	X̄ score for blacks = 12.8 X̄ score for whites = 14.4	Three-item political trust index	X̄ score for blacks = 10.0 X̄ score for whites = 11.2
...ur-item ...vernment ...essibility ...ex	X̄ score for blacks = 14.3 X̄ score for whites = 14.2		
...o items	68% of blacks said they could do something to affect a local government decision; 76% of whites said they could do something. 73% of blacks said their parents could do something to affect a local government decision; 91% of whites said their parents could do something.	Two items	61% of blacks said the mayor is honest; 76% of whites said he is honest. 61% of blacks said the police are honest; 81% of whites.
...o items	31% of blacks said government cared what family thinks; 41% of whites said government cared. 43% of blacks disagreed family had no say about what government does; 53% of whites disagreed.	Two items	46% of blacks said policemen could be trusted; 74% of whites. Blacks less trusting than whites toward all authority figures, except toward elected black political leaders.

(continued)

RESEARCH REPORTED[a]	DATE OF SURVEY	RESEARCH SITE	GRADES SAMPLED	SAMPLE SIZE
Bachman (personal communication)	Spring 1968	National sample (panel survey)	11 (including boys out of school)	138 blacks (weighted N); 1576 whites (weighted N)
Greenberg (1969)	Spring 1968	Philadelphia, Pennsylvania	3,5,7,8	401 blacks; 462 whites
Williams (1972, 1974)	Spring 1968	Cobb County; Oconee County; Americus, Georgia	3,6,9	576 blacks; 1508 whites
Krause (1972) (plus personal communication)	April-May 1968	Chicago, Glenview, Northbrook, Illinois	6-8	48 inner-city blacks; 123 inner-city Spanish-Americans; 120 inner-city whites; 106 suburban whites

(continued)

Measure of Sense of Political Efficacy[b]	Finding about Efficacy	Measure of Political Trust[b]	Finding about Trust
		Three-item political trust scale	$\bar{X}$ score for black = 3.51 $\bar{X}$ score for whites = 3.52
		Two items	54% of blacks said government in Washington could be trusted; 65% of whites. 40% of blacks said the government almost never makes mistakes; 37% of whites said the government almost never makes mistakes.
...e-item ...ex	29% of blacks scored high or very high; 43% of whites scored high or very high.	Two items	51% of blacks believed the president is more honest than most men; 31% of whites believed the president is more honest. 15% of blacks said the U.S. government never makes a mistake; 3% of whites said the U.S. government never makes a mistake.
...ree-item ...icacy ...ward ...esident ...dex	No significant racial differences.	Three-item trust toward president index	No significant racial differences.
...ree-item ...icacy ...ward ...ayor ...dex	Suburban whites most efficacious; inner-city blacks and Spanish-Americans least efficacious.	Three-item trust toward mayor index	Suburban whites most trusting; inner-city blacks least trusting.

(continued)

RESEARCH REPORTED[a]	DATE OF SURVEY	RESEARCH SITE	GRADES SAMPLED	SAMPLE SIZE
Stevens (1969) (plus personal communication)	May 1968	Frederick County, Maryland	5–8	137 blacks; 322 whites
Lyons (1970)	October–December 1968	Toledo, Ohio	5–12	847 blacks; 1468 whites (data for political efficacy based on 752 blacks; 1293 whites)
Vaillancourt (1972)	December 1968 (panel survey)	Berkeley, Oakland, California	4,6,8	143 blacks; 137 whites

(continued)

Measure of Sense of Political Efficacy[b]	Finding about Efficacy	Measure of Political Trust[b]	Finding about Trust
hree-item fficacy oward olice index	Suburban whites most efficacious; inner-city blacks least efficacious.	Three-item trust toward police index	Suburban whites most trusting.
ight-item olitical fficacy cale	22% of blacks scored high; 41% of whites scored high.		
ive-item ndex	32% of blacks scored high; 47% of whites scored high.	Five-item political cynicism index	27% of blacks scored low on political cynicism; 41% of whites scored low.
		Three items	$\bar{X}$ presidential affect for blacks on whether president keeps his promises = 4.14 $\bar{X}$ presidential affect for whites on whether president keeps his promises = 4.24
			$\bar{X}$ presidential affect for blacks on whether president is honest = 4.15 $\bar{X}$ presidential affect for whites on whether president is honest = 4.34
			$\bar{X}$ presidential affect for blacks on whether president makes mistakes = 4.01

(continued)

RESEARCH REPORTED[a]	DATE OF SURVEY	RESEARCH SITE	GRADES SAMPLED	SAMPLE SIZE
Vaillancourt (1972)	Late January 1969 (panel survey)	Berkeley, Oakland, California	4,6,8	143 blacks; 137 whites
Ehman (1969, 1972) (plus personal communication)	February 1969	Pontiac, Michigan (panel survey)	12	41 blacks; 62 whites
Heinz (1971) (plus personal communication)	Blacks sampled March 1969; Whites sampled January 1968.	All-black high school in Chicago, Illinois; All-white high school in York Township, Illinois (suburb west of Chicago).	10–12	About 500 blacks; about 400 whites

(continued)

Measure of Sense of Political Efficacy[b]	Finding about Efficacy	Measure of Political Trust[b]	Finding about Trust
			$\bar{X}$ presidential affect for whites on whether president makes mistakes = 4.04
		Three items	$\bar{X}$ presidential affect for blacks on whether president keeps his promises = 3.63 $\bar{X}$ presidential affect for whites on whether president keeps his promises = 4.41
			$\bar{X}$ presidential affect for blacks on whether president is honest = 3.83 $\bar{X}$ presidential affect for whites on whether president is honest = 4.42
			$\bar{X}$ presidential affect for blacks on whether president makes mistakes = 3.78 $\bar{X}$ presidential affect for whites on whether president makes mistakes = 4.31
Four-item political efficacy scale	$\bar{X}$ score for blacks = 3.10 $\bar{X}$ score for whites = 2.93	Four-item political cynicism scale	$\bar{X}$ trust score for blacks = 2.76 $\bar{X}$ trust score for whites = 3.53
		Five items	39% of blacks did not agree that the people who make the laws don't understand what is happening today; 76% of whites did not agree.

(continued)

RESEARCH REPORTED[a]	DATE OF SURVEY	RESEARCH SITE	GRADES SAMPLED	SAMPLE SIZE
Bachman (personal communication)	Spring 1969	National sample (panel survey)	12 (including boys not in school)	204 blacks (weighted N); 1611 whites (weighted N)
Vaillancourt (1972)	May-June 1969 (panel survey for trust items)	Berkeley, Oakland, California	4,6,8	Efficacy sample: 160 blacks; 190 whites. Trust sample: 143 blacks; 137 whites.

(continued)

Measure of Sense of Political Efficacy[b]	Finding about Efficacy	Measure of Political Trust[b]	Finding about Trust
			68% of blacks did not agree that laws are for the good of the few; 93% of whites did not agree.
			43% of blacks did not agree that the laws treat the poor worse; 80% of whites did not agree.
			10% of blacks said most police are honest; 63% of whites said most police are honest.
			18% of blacks said the typical policeman does a good job; 54% of whites said he does a good job.
		Three-item political trust scale	$\bar{X}$ score for blacks = 3.37 $\bar{X}$ score for whites = 3.49
Five-item index	23% of blacks scored medium high or high; 42% of whites scored medium high or high.	Three items	$\bar{X}$ presidential affect for blacks on whether president keeps his promises = 3.42 $\bar{X}$ presidential affect for whites on whether president keeps his promises = 3.97
			$\bar{X}$ presidential affect for blacks on whether president is honest = 3.52 $\bar{X}$ presidential affect for whites on whether president is honest = 4.10
			$\bar{X}$ presidential affect for blacks on whether president makes mistakes = 3.58

(continued)

RESEARCH REPORTED[a]	DATE OF SURVEY	RESEARCH SITE	GRADES SAMPLED	SAMPLE SIZE
Liebschutz and Niemi (1974) (plus personal communication)	June 1969	Rochester, New York	3–8	551 blacks; 139 whites
Rodgers (1972, 1974); Rodgers and Lewis (1974) (plus personal communication)	Fall 1969	Edgecombe County, North Carolina	10–12	371 blacks; 280 whites
Rodgers and Taylor (1971) (plus personal communication)	Late 1969; early 1970	Charleston, South Carolina	9–12	106 blacks; 198 whites
Strauss (1973) (plus personal communication)	Spring 1970	New York metropolitan area	10–12	115 blacks; 1030 whites

(continued)

Measure of Sense of Political Efficacy[b]	Finding about Efficacy	Measure of Political Trust[b]	Finding about Trust
			$\overline{X}$ presidential affect for whites on whether president makes mistakes = 3.97
Five-item index	$\overline{X}$ score for blacks = 8.20 $\overline{X}$ score for whites = 9.23		
Three-item index	25% of blacks scored high; 22% of whites scored high.	Five-item political cynicism index, plus item about police	71% of blacks scored medium or low on political cynicism; 64% of whites scored medium or low. 61% of blacks said police as or more honest than most men; 86% of whites said police as or more honest.
		Five-item political trust index, plus item about police	71% of blacks scored medium or high on political trust; 79% of whites scored medium or high. 53% of blacks said police as or more honest than most men; 81% of whites said police as or more honest.
Single item	27% of blacks disagreed politics and government were too complicated to understand; 29% of whites disagreed.	Single item	27% of blacks said most or some governmental leaders were honest; 49% of whites said most or some leaders were honest.

(continued)

RESEARCH REPORTED[a]	DATE OF SURVEY	RESEARCH SITE	GRADES SAMPLED	SAMPLE SIZE
Hulbary (1972, 1974) (plus personal communication)	May-June 1970	North Judson, Muncie, Hammond, Indiana; Chicago, Illinois	9–12 (plus some high school graduates)	88 blacks; 98 whites
Bachman (personal communication)	Summer 1970	National sample (panel survey)	1st year college (including men not in school)	198 blacks (weighted N); 1601 whites (weighted N)
Sears (1975)	February 1971	Fresno, California	Ages 9 to 14	About 265 blacks; about 390 whites
Carmines (1972) (plus personal communication)	Spring 1971	Hampton, Virginia	7–9	224 blacks; 197 whites
Funderburk (1973) (plus personal communication)	May 1971	Key Largo, Florida	4–12	57 blacks; 679 whites

(continued)

MEASURE OF SENSE OF POLITICAL EFFICACY[b]	FINDING ABOUT EFFICACY	MEASURE OF POLITICAL TRUST[b]	FINDING ABOUT TRUST
Three-item political powerlessness scale	$\bar{X}$ powerfulness score for blacks = −.31 $\bar{X}$ powerfulness score for whites = +.29		
		Three items political trust scale	$\bar{X}$ score for blacks = 3.17 $\bar{X}$ score for whites = 3.26
		Three items	40% of blacks said policemen could be trusted; 76% of whites said policemen could be trusted. 65% of blacks said the government did not often or usually make mistakes; 76% of whites said the government did not often or usually make mistakes. 75% of blacks said the president did not often make mistakes; 80% of whites said the president did not often make mistakes.
Five-item scale	32% of blacks scored high; 42% of whites scored high.		
Four-item index	Blacks less efficacious than whites ($r = -.10$)	Four-item scale	Race not related to trust in government.

(continued)

RESEARCH REPORTED[a]	DATE OF SURVEY	RESEARCH SITE	GRADES SAMPLED	SAMPLE SIZE
Jaros and Kolson (1974) (plus personal communication)	May 1971	Rural communities near Middle-field, Ohio (Geauga County)	4–8	43 blacks; 70 Amish whites; 151 non-Amish whites
Orum and Cohen (1973) (plus personal communication)	Spring and Fall 1971	East St. Louis, Chicago, Chicago Heights, Park Forest, Illinois	4–6	145 blacks; 295 whites
			7–12	492 blacks; 469 whites
Button (1972, 1974)	October 1971– January 1972	Austin, Texas	12	68 blacks; 103 whites
Remy (personal communication)	Winter 1971	Students from all 50 states who attended a nongovern-mental educa-tional pro-gram in Wash-ington, D.C.	12	97 blacks; 1368 whites

(continued)

Measure of Sense of Political Efficacy[b]	Finding about Efficacy	Measure of Political Trust[b]	Finding about Trust
		Single item	35% of blacks said the president was more honest than most men; 46% of Amish whites said the president was more honest; 24% of non-Amish whites said the president was more honest.
		Three-item political cynicism scale	$\bar{X}$ trust score for blacks = 1.15 $\bar{X}$ trust score for whites = 1.86
		Five-item political cynicism scale	$\bar{X}$ trust score for blacks = 2.43 $\bar{X}$ trust score for whites = 3.41
Eight-item efficacy scale	$\bar{X}$ score for blacks = 18.70 $\bar{X}$ score for whites = 20.64	Five-item political cynicism scale	$\bar{X}$ trust score for blacks = 9.57 $\bar{X}$ trust score for whites = 10.19
Two-item ability to help solve local and national problems scale	$\bar{X}$ score for blacks = 4.26 $\bar{X}$ score for whites = 5.18		
Eleven items	22% of blacks disagreed that politics and government seemed too complicated to understand; 39% of whites disagreed.	Five items	46% of blacks agreed they usually had confidence the government will do what is right; 50% of whites agreed.
	73% of blacks disagreed that people like me don't have any say about what the government does; 81% of whites disagreed.		21% of blacks disagreed that politicians don't really mean what they say; 37% of whites disagreed.

(continued)

RESEARCH REPORTED[a]	DATE OF SURVEY	RESEARCH SITE	GRADES SAMPLED	SAMPLE SIZE
Long (April 1974, December 1975) (plus personal communication)	May 1972	Cairo, Illinois; Cape Girardeau, Missouri; Paducah, Kentucky	7–12	About 330 blacks; about 1250 whites
Barger (1974) (plus personal communication)	April 1973	San Antonio, Texas, metropolitan area	Elementary school	123 blacks; 303 whites
Jennings (personal communication)	April 1973	National sample (questionnaires)	12	About 2270 blacks; about 13,680 whites

(continued)

MEASURE OF SENSE OF POLITICAL EFFICACY[b]	FINDING ABOUT EFFICACY	MEASURE OF POLITICAL TRUST[b]	FINDING ABOUT TRUST
	84% of blacks agreed that people like me can change what happens in the government; 80% of whites agreed.		25% of blacks agreed that when the going gets tough the President can be trusted to level with the American people; 29% of whites agreed.
	Blacks less efficacious than whites on five of the eight items measuring influence on foreign policy and world affairs; Negligible racial differences on three items.		43% of blacks disagreed that Congress can't be trusted to represent the people fairly; 58% of whites disagreed.
			46% of blacks disagreed that the courts can't be trusted to give a person a fair hearing; 70% of whites disagreed.
Olsen's Political Incapability Scale (4 items)	$\bar{X}$ capability score for blacks = 14.0 $\bar{X}$ capability score for whites = 15.5	Olsen's Political Discontentment Scale (4 items)	$\bar{X}$ contentment score for blacks = 15.7 $\bar{X}$ contentment score for whites = 16.8
		Two items	31% of blacks agreed the president is very honest; 52% of whites agreed.
			57% of blacks agreed the police are very honest; 75% of whites agreed.
Four items	29% of blacks disagreed that voting is only way people have a say about what the government does; 37% of whites disagreed.	Five items	40% of blacks said the government in Washington could be trusted to do the right thing about all the time or most of the time;

(continued)

RESEARCH REPORTED[a]	DATE OF SURVEY	RESEARCH SITE	GRADES SAMPLED	SAMPLE SIZE
Long (August 1974)	May 1973	Fayette County, Kentucky	7–12	About 105 blacks; about 850 whites

(continued)

Measure of Sense of Political Efficacy[b]	Finding about Efficacy	Measure of Political Trust[b]	Finding about Trust
	21% of blacks disagreed that government is too complicated to understand; 21% of whites disagreed.		61% of whites said the government could be trusted to do the right thing.
	61% of blacks disagreed that their family has no say about what the government does; 62% of whites disagreed.		34% of blacks said not very many or hardly any people running the government are crooked; 39% of whites said not very many or hardly any are crooked.
	40% of blacks disagreed that public officials don't care what people like me think; 40% of whites disagreed.		37% of blacks said the government doesn't waste much or wastes only some tax money; 41% of whites said the government doesn't waste much or wastes only some money.
			42% of blacks said that almost all the people running the government usually know what they are doing; 61% of whites said they usually know what they are doing.
			33% of blacks said the government was run for the benefit of all; 37% of whites said the government was run for the benefit of all.
Olsen's Political Incapability Scale (4 items)	$\bar{X}$ z-scores on political capability for blacks = $-.395$ $\bar{X}$ z-scores on political capability for whites = $-.004$	Olsen's Political Discontentment Scale (4 items)	$\bar{X}$ z-scores on political contentment for blacks = $-.356$ $\bar{X}$ z-scores on political contentment for whites = $-.023$

(continued)

RESEARCH REPORTED[a]	DATE OF SURVEY	RESEARCH SITE	GRADES SAMPLED	SAMPLE SIZE
Hershey (personal communicaiton)	November 1973– February 1974	Stratified random sample of Florida public schools	4,6,8, 10,12	514 blacks; 1213 whites
Campbell (personal communication)	November 1973– March 1974	Atlanta metropolitan area	12	367 blacks; 568 whites
Foster (1976) (plus personal communication)	March, May 1974	Peoria, East St. Louis, Illinois	4,6,8, 10,12	332 blacks; 347 whites
Barger (1974) (plus personal communication)	April 1974	San Antonio, Texas, metropolitan area	Elementary school	106 blacks; 233 whites
			Middle school	98 blacks; 67 whites
			Senior high school	98 blacks; 113 whites

(continued)

Measure of Sense of Political Efficacy[b]	Finding about Efficacy	Measure of Political Trust[b]	Finding about Trust
Two-item index	27% of blacks scored high; 36% of whites scored high.		
		Three-item political trust scale	$\bar{X}$ score for blacks = 2.84 $\bar{X}$ score for whites = 3.26
Five-item index	8% of blacks scored high; 26% of whites scored high.	Two items	24% of blacks said the president was as or more honest than most men; 60% of whites said the president was as or more honest.
			10% of blacks said the mayor was as or more honest than most men; 31% of whites said the mayor was as or more honest.
		Two items	16% of blacks agreed the president is very honest; 10% of whites agreed.
			51% of blacks agreed the police are very honest; 52% of whites agreed.
		Two items	6% of blacks agreed the president is very honest; 12% of whites agreed.
			9% of blacks agreed the police are very honest; 32% of whites agreed.
		Two items	2% of blacks agreed the president is very honest; 8% of whites agreed.

(continued)

RESEARCH REPORTED[a]	DATE OF SURVEY	RESEARCH SITE	GRADES SAMPLED	SAMPLE SIZE
Long (March 1975, August 1975, July 1976)	December 1974	St. Louis, Missouri, inner-city schools	9–12	About 370 blacks; about 550 whites
Long (personal communication)	May 1975	Evansville, Indiana	9–12	31 blacks; 417 whites

Measure of Sense of Political Efficacy[b]	Finding about Efficacy	Measure of Political Trust[b]	Finding about Trust
			8% of blacks agreed the police are very honest; 27% of whites agreed.
Olsen's Political Incapability Scale (4 items)	$\bar{X}$ z-scores on political capability for blacks = +.03 $\bar{X}$ z-scores on political capability for whites = −.05	Olsen's Political Discontentment Scale (4 items)	$\bar{X}$ z-scores on political contentment for blacks = −.01 $\bar{X}$ z-scores on political contentment for whites = +.02
		Agger's Political Cynicism Scale (6 items)	$\bar{X}$ z-scores on political trust for blacks = +.07 $\bar{X}$ z-scores on political trust for whites = −.04
Olsen's Political Incapability Scale (4 items)	$\bar{X}$ capability score for blacks = 11.52 $\bar{X}$ capability score for whites = 11.97	Olsen's Political Discontentment Scale (4 items)	$\bar{X}$ contentment score for blacks = 11.13 $\bar{X}$ contentment score for whites = 11.51
		Agger's Political Cynicism Scale (6 items)	$\bar{X}$ trust score for blacks = 17.94 $\bar{X}$ trust score for whites = 17.78

he full citation for these sources, see Bibliography, Part 1.
a detailed report on the items and scoring procedures used to construct these measures, see Appendix C.

APPENDIX B

Research Sites Where Feelings of
Political Efficacy and Political Trust
Were Measured among Black and
White Schoolchildren

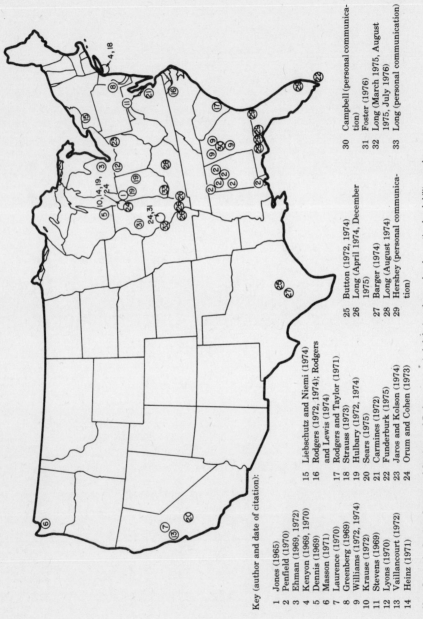

Key (author and date of citation):

1 Jones (1965)
2 Penfield (1970)
3 Ehman (1969, 1972)
4 Kenyon (1969, 1970)
5 Dennis (1969)
6 Masson (1971)
7 Laurence (1970)
8 Greenberg (1969)
9 Williams (1972, 1974)
10 Krause (1972)
11 Stevens (1969)
12 Lyons (1970)
13 Vaillancourt (1972)
14 Heinz (1971)

15 Liebschutz and Niemi (1974)
16 Rodgers (1972, 1974); Rodgers
    and Lewis (1974)
17 Rodgers and Taylor (1971)
18 Strauss (1973)
19 Hulbary (1972, 1974)
20 Sears (1975)
21 Carmines (1972)
22 Funderburk (1975)
23 Jaros and Kolson (1974)
24 Orum and Cohen (1973)

25 Button (1972, 1974)
26 Long (April 1974, December
    1975)
27 Barger (1974)
28 Long (August 1974)
29 Hershey (personal communica-
    tion)

30 Campbell (personal communica-
    tion)
31 Foster (1976)
32 Long (March 1975, August
    1975, July 1976)
33 Long (personal communication)

NOTE: Surveys by Jennings, Langton and Jennings, and Bachman are not included, since they are based on national probability samples. Remy's study is not included since it surveyed students from all 50 states.

APPENDIX C

Measures of Sense of Political Efficacy and Political Trust

The following list of questions begins with the political efficacy items employed by David Easton and Jack Dennis and the political cynicism items employed by Kenneth P. Langton and M. Kent Jennings. Their questions are cited first because they have been widely employed by subsequent researchers. The remaining questions follow the same order as the listing of findings reported in Appendix A.

Although, as we noted above (see p. 19), the terms index and scale technically have different meanings, throughout this book we have employed the terminology used by the authors of the research reports. Most of the authors who used the term *scale* employed some procedure to demonstrate the unidimensionality of their items. I briefly report on the scaling procedures used to construct these measures. Where authors reported using an *index*, they usually made no attempt to demonstrate unidimensionality, but in those cases where some tests were used I report these procedures.

As we mentioned above, researchers have often used weak tests of unidimensionality. I do not specifically critique these tests, but reporting these procedures does not constitute an endorsement.

Political Efficacy Items used by David Easton and Jack Dennis:[1]

1. "Voting is the only way that people like my mother and father can have any say about how the government runs things."

148

2. "Sometimes I can't understand what goes on in the government."

3. "What happens in the government will happen no matter what people do. It is like the weather, there is nothing people can do about it."

4. "There are some big powerful men in the government who are running the whole thing and they do not care about us ordinary people."

5. "My family doesn't have any say about what the government does."

6. "I don't think people in the government care much what people like my family think."

7. "Citizens don't have a chance to say what they think about running the government."

8. "How much do these people [the average person] *help decide which laws are made for our country:* Very much, Some, Very Little, or Not at all?"

For the first seven items, a disagree response was scored as efficacious. Based upon a factor analysis to identify the principal components of sense of political efficacy, Easton and Dennis selected items 3, 4, 5, 6, and 7 to build their index of sense of political efficacy.

Six-item Political Cynicism Scale developed by Kenneth P. Langton and M. Kent Jennings:[2]

1. "Over the years, how much attention do you feel the government pays to what the people think when it decides what to do—a good deal, some, or not much?"

2. "Do you think that quite a few of the people running the government are a little crooked, not very many are, or do you think that hardly any of them are?"

3. "Do you think that people in the government waste a lot of the money we pay in taxes, waste some of it, or don't waste very much of it?"

4. "How much of the time do you think you can trust the government in Washington to do what is right—just about always, most of the time, or only some of the time?"

5. "Do you feel that almost all of the people running the government are smart people who usually know what they are doing, or do you think that quite a few of them don't seem to know what they are doing?"

6. "Would you say the government is pretty much run by a few big

interests looking out for themselves or that it is run for the benefit of all the people?"

Langton and Jennings report that these items formed a Guttman scale with a coefficient of reproducibility (CR) of .92.

These items can be used to measure either political cynicism or political trust. For example, Jennings and Richard G. Niemi used items 2 through 6 to construct a political trust scale.[3]

Political Efficacy Item used by James T. Jones:[4]

"People like me and my parents don't have any say about what the government of our city does." Disagreement was considered efficacious.

Political Efficacy Items used in the University of Michigan Survey Research Center's 1965 questionnaire.[5]

Jennings used items 1 and 6 employed by Easton and Dennis, plus the following adaptation of item 2:

"Sometimes politics and government seem so complicated that a person like me can't really understand what's going on. Agree strongly Agree somewhat   Disagree somewhat   Disagree strongly."

Political Trust Items used in the University of Michigan Survey Research Center's 1965 questionnaire:[6]

Jennings used items 4, 2, 3, 5, and 6 employed in the Langton and Jennings political cynicism scale.

Two-item Political Efficacy Scale developed by Langton and Jennings:[7]

Langton and Jennings used item 1 employed by Easton and Dennis, plus an adaptation of item 2 (see the Michigan SRC questionnaire wording above). For both items, a disagree response was scored as efficacious. Langton and Jennings reported that these items formed a Guttman scale with a CR of .94.

Three-item Political Trust Scale developed by Jerald G. Bachman:[8]

1. "Do you think the government wastes much of the money we pay in taxes? Nearly all tax money is wasted. A lot of tax money is

wasted. Some tax money is wasted. A little tax money is wasted. No tax money is wasted."

2. "How much of the time do you think you can trust the government in Washington to do what is right? Almost always   Often   Sometimes   Seldom   Never."

3. "Do you feel that the people running the government are smart people who usually know what they are doing? They almost always know what they are doing. They usually know what they are doing. They sometimes know what they are doing. They seldom know what they are doing. They never know what they are doing."

Bachman used these items to build an additive measure of political trust, but does not explicity discuss his scaling procedures. His measure ranges from a possible low of 1.0 to a possible high of 5.0.

Political Efficacy Items used by Henry I. Penfield, Jr.:[9]

Penfield used items 1 and 5 employed by Easton and Dennis, and the same adaptation of item 2 employed by Langton and Jennings. In addition, he used item 1 of the Langton and Jennings political cynicism scale, which he considered a measure of sense of political effectiveness.

Five-item Political Cynicism Scale developed by Penfield:[10]

Penfield adapted items 2 through 6 employed by Langton and Jennings. One set of questions aimed at attitudes toward the national government, the other set toward the government of Alabama. Penfield reports that the CRs for the cynicism scales were always above .80 and usually close to .90. He notes, however, that Guttman scaling procedures usually require a CR of .90.

Four-item Political Efficacy Scale developed by Lee H. Ehman:[11]

1. "When we become adults, we won't have much influence on what the government does.
Strongly Agree   Agree   Undecided   Disagree   Strongly Disagree."

2. "I don't think public officials care much what people like me think."

3. "Sometimes politics and government seem so complicated that a person like me can't really understand what's going on."

4. "Voting is the only way people like me will have any say about how the government runs things."

For all these items a disagree response was scored as efficacious. Ehman reports that these items formed a Guttman scale with a CR of .903. Scores ranged from 1.0 to 5.0.

Four-item Political Cynicism Scale developed by Ehman:[12]

Ehman used items 2, 4, 5, and 6 of the Langton and Jennings political cynicism scale. He reports that these items formed a Guttman scale with a CR of .928. Scores ranged from 1.0 to 5.0. In presenting his data I reversed the direction of his scores, so that high scores in Appendix A indicate political trust.

Three-item Political Efficacy Index used by Sandra J. Kenyon:[13]

1. "After you become twenty-one, do you feel you will be able to have as much say about what the government does as most people do?"
2. "How well would you say you understand the important issues facing this country—not as well as most people your age, as well as most people your age, or better than most people your age?"
3. "Would you say that voting is the *only* way that people like you and your family can have any say about how the government runs things, or do you think there are other ways open to people like you?" (Disagreement scored as efficacious.)

Seven-item Political Cynicism Scale developed by Kenyon:[14]

Kenyon slightly modified items 1, 2, 3, and 6 used by Langton and Jennings, and added the following three items:
1. "Do you think that almost all the people running the government try to treat everybody equally, or do you think that quite a few of them treat people unequally?"
2. "Would you say that you can trust the people in the government to tell the truth almost all the time, only sometimes, or almost never?"
3. "Would you say that quite a few of the people running the government work hard at their jobs, or do you think that quite a few of them do as little work as they can get away with?"

Kenyon reports that all these items scaled according to the critical ratio test. Critical ratios ranged from 2.58 to 7.82.

Four-item Government Responsiveness Index developed by Jack Dennis:[15]

Dennis used item 6 employed by Easton and Dennis, and added the following three items:

1. "I don't think that people in the government care much what people like me think."

2. "I don't think that people in the state government in Madison care much what people like my family think."

3. "I don't think that people in the city government care much what people like my family think."

For all these items, a disagree response was scored as efficacious. These items were selected for the index through a factor analysis (principal component analysis with a varimax rotation) for 45 items. The rotated factor loadings for these items on the responsiveness component ranged from .58 to .79. The range of scores for the index was not reported.

Four-item Government Accessibility Index developed by Dennis:[16]

1. "If the Governor of Wisconsin did something I didn't like, I would feel free to complain to him about it."

2. "If the mayor of Milwaukee did something I didn't like, I would feel free to complain to him about it."

3. "If a policeman did something I didn't like, I would feel free to complain to him about it."

4. "If I wanted to, I could get someone in the Milwaukee city government to listen to what I want."

For all these items, an agree response was scored as efficacious. These items were selected for the index through a factor analysis for 45 items. The rotated factor loadings on the accessibility component ranged from .56 to .87. The range of scores for the index was not reported.

Three-item Political Trust Index developed by Dennis:[17]

1. "Quite a few of the people running the government are dishonest."

2. "Quite a few politicians are dishonest."

3. "Most of the people who try to get elected to public office can be trusted to do what is right."

These items were selected for the index through a factor analysis for 45 items. The rotated factor loadings on the trust component ranged from .42 to .78. The range of scores for the index was not reported.

Political Efficacy Items used by Jack K. Masson:[18]

1. "Suppose that one day some men came into a park you usually play in and started cutting down the trees and told all the children that there wouldn't be a park there any more. Is there anything you could do to save the park in order for children to keep playing there? (Probe for what they could do.)"

2. "Is there anything your mother or father could do to save the park? (Probe for what they could do.)"

3. "Suppose there was a street crossing in your neighborhood where a lot of people have been struck by cars. If your parents should want to have a traffic light and wait and walk signal put in at this crossing who should they ask to do it?"

4. (If the child's answer was a government official, he was asked the next question. If not, he was told the correct answer was the city engineering department and then asked the question.) "If [respondent's answer or the supplied answer] didn't think it was a good idea to put in a traffic light, what could your parents do in order to get him to change his mind?"

The data reported in Appendix A are based upon the responses to the first two of these items.

Political Trust Items used by Masson:[19]

1. "Both parents and teachers tell children to be honest and always tell the truth. Now I want to ask you about whether certain grown-ups are always honest and always tell the truth. Do you think policemen are always honest and tell the truth?   1) yes   2) no   3) don't know."

2. "What about the mayor of Seattle?   1) yes   2) no   3) don't know."

Political Efficacy Items used by Joan E. Laurence:[20]

1. "People in the government care about what people like my family think." (Agreement considered efficacious.)

Plus item 5 used by Easton and Dennis.

Laurence did not present a verbatim report of the items she used to measure political trust.

Political Trust Items used by Edward S. Greenberg:[21]

1. "The government in Washington can be trusted. Do you think that this statement is ... True ... False ... I don't know."

2. "What do you think of the government? Circle the number of the statement in each line that best describes the government. . . .

(1) The government almost never makes mistakes (2) The government makes lots of mistakes (3) I don't know."

Five-item Political Efficacy Index used by Thomas J. Williams:[22]

Williams used items 3, 4, 5, 6, and 7 employed by Easton and Dennis.

Political Trust Items used by Williams:[23]

1. "Place a check mark or an X by the statement which best fits your views. The President is more honest than most men. The President is as honest as most men. The President is less honest than most men."

2. "The Government of the United States: Never makes a mistake. Sometimes makes a mistake. Almost always makes mistakes."

Three-item Efficacy toward the President Index developed by Merton S. Krause:[24]

1. "It would take so much time, effort or money to influence the President that it just wouldn't be worth it for a person like me.
    Strongly Agree Agree Disagree Strongly Disagree."

2. "A person like me would never get a chance even to try to influence the President."

3. "Suppose the President was considering doing something you thought was harmful or unjust. A person like you could do something about it."

For items 1 and 2 a disagree response was scored as efficacious. For item 3 agreement was scored as efficacious. In constructing this index, item 3 was double weighted.

Three-item Efficacy toward the Mayor Index developed by Krause:[25]

1. "It would take so much time, effort or money for a person like me to influence the mayor that it just wouldn't be worth trying.
    Strongly Agree Agree Disagree Strongly Disagree."

2. "People like me would never get a chance to be heard by the mayor."

3. "Suppose the mayor was considering doing something you

thought was harmful or unjust. In general a person like you could do something about it."

For items 1 and 2 a disagree response was scored as efficacious. For item 3 agreement was scored as efficacious. In constructing this index, item 3 was double weighted.

Three-item Efficacy toward Police Index developed by Krause:[26]

1. "People who try to argue or disagree with policemen are wasting their time or worse.
    Strongly Agree   Agree   Disagree   Strongly Disagree."
2. "Suppose you were near a place where a crime had been committed, and a policeman saw you. Most policemen would give you a chance to explain before they did anything."
3. "If I was stopped for some traffic violation, there would be no use for me to tell the policeman what really happened, most policemen have already made up their minds."

For items 1 and 3 a disagree response was scored as efficacious. For item 2 agreement was scored as efficacious. In constructing this index, item 2 was double weighted.

Three-item Trust toward President Index developed by Krause:[27]

1. "The President is more interested in helping the people than in getting re-elected.
    Strongly Agree   Agree   Disagree   Strongly Disagree."
2. "Suppose a group of people were being hurt by the draft. The President would not try to give them fair and considerate treatment."
3. "In general the President is the kind of person who does what he promises to do."

For items 1 and 3 agreement was scored as trust. For item 2 a disagree response was scored as trust. In constructing this index, item 2 was double weighted.

Three-item Trust toward Mayor Index developed by Krause:[28]

1. "The mayor would try to do what is best for the people even if it costs him his re-election.
    Strongly Agree   Agree   Disagree   Strongly Disagree."
2. "Suppose a group of people were being hurt by being made to

move for urban renewal. I would expect that the mayor would *not* treat them fairly and give serious consideration to their problem."

3. "On the whole, the mayor is honest."

For items 1 and 3 agreement was scored as trust. For item 2 a disagree response was scored as trust. In constructing this index, item 2 was double weighted.

Three-item Trust toward Police Index developed by Krause:[29]

1. "Suppose you were in a car that was rushing to the hospital for an emergency, and a policeman stopped you. Once the policeman knew your reason for speeding, you would expect him to assist you.
    Strongly Agree   Agree   Disagree   Strongly Disagree."
2. "If I asked a policeman for help, in general I would not expect him to try very hard to help me."
3. "Very few policemen will do favors for money."

For items 1 and 3 agreement was scored as trust. For item 2 a disagree response was scored as trust. In constructing this index, item 2 was double weighted.

Political Efficacy Scale developed by Alden J. Stevens:[30]

Stevens used all eight efficacy items asked by Easton and Dennis. He reports that they yielded a reliability coefficient of .99 using the Kuder-Richardson Formula 21.

Five-item Political Efficacy Index used by Schley R. Lyons:[31]

Lyons used items 3, 4, 5, 6, and 7 employed by Easton and Dennis.

Five-item Political Cynicism Index used by Lyons:[32]

Lyons used items 2 through 6 employed by Langton and Jennings.

Political Trust Items used by Pauline Marie Vaillancourt:[33]

"Think of the *President* as he really is...
1. "(1) Always keeps his promises (2) Almost always keeps his

promises (3) Usually keeps his promises (4) Sometimes does not keep his promises (5) Usually does not keep his promises (6) Almost never keeps his promises . . .

2. "(1) More honest than almost anyone (2) More honest than most people (3) More honest than some people (4) More dishonest than some people (5) More dishonest than most people (6) More dishonest than almost anyone . . .

3. "(1) Almost never makes mistakes (2) Rarely makes mistakes (3) Sometimes makes mistakes (4) Often makes mistakes (5) Usually makes mistakes (6) Almost always makes mistakes . . ."

Vaillancourt's scores ranged from 1.0 (positive affect) to 6.0 (negative affect). In presenting her data I reversed the direction of her scores, so that high scores in Appendix A indicate political trust.

Five-item Political Efficacy Index used by Vaillancourt:[34]

Vaillancourt used items 3, 4, 5, 6, and 7 employed by Easton and Dennis.

Political Trust Items used by Anne M. Heinz:[35]

1. "People who make the laws don't understand what is happening today."
2. "Laws are made for the good of a few."
3. "In general, policemen are honest."
4. "How well do you think the typical policeman does his job?"

Five-item Political Efficacy Index used by Sarah F. Liebschutz and Richard G. Niemi:[36]

Liebschutz and Niemi used items 3, 4, 5, 6, and 7 employed by Easton and Dennis. Scores on their index ranged from 1.0 to 16.0.

Three-item Political Efficacy Index developed by Harrell R. Rodgers, Jr.:[37]

Rodgers used items 4, 5, and 6 employed by Easton and Dennis. Rodgers asked all five questions employed in the Easton and Dennis political efficacy index. Through a factor analysis (Kaiser's varimax solution with orthogonal rotation) he concluded that items 4, 5, and 6 measured a single dimension and that items 3 and 7 should not be included in his index.

Five-item Political Cynicism Index developed by Rodgers:[38]

Rodgers used items 2 through 6 employed by Langton and Jennings. Through a factor analysis he concluded that these items measured a single dimension.

Trust in Police Item used by Rodgers and Edward B. Lewis:[39]

"How honest do you think the police are compared to most men? More honest . . . As honest . . . Less honest . . . Don't know."

Five-item Political Trust Index developed by Rodgers and George Taylor:[40]

Rodgers and Taylor used items 2 through 6 employed by Langton and Jennings. Through a factor analysis (Kaiser's varimax solution with orthogonal rotation) they concluded that these items measured a single dimension.

Trust in Policemen Item used by Rodgers and Taylor:[41]

Rodgers and Taylor used the same item employed by Rodgers and Edwards.

Political Efficacy Item used by George H. Strauss:[42]

"Sometimes politics and government seem so complicated that I can't really understand what's going on."

Strauss did not consider this item to be a measure of sense of political efficacy, but argued that it measured "understandability of politics." However, this item has been used as a component of the political efficacy index in numerous studies, and we report it as an efficacy measure to maintain comparability with other analyses.

Political Trust Item used by Strauss:[43]

"How many of governmental and political leaders in the U.S. are honest and sincere? Most of them. Some of them. A few of them. None of them. Don't know."

Three-item Political Powerlessness Scale developed by William E. Hulbary:[44]

1. "It is difficult for people to have much control over the things politicians do in office."
2. "As far as world affairs are concerned, most of us are the victims of forces we can neither understand nor control."
3. "This world is run by the few people in power and there is not much the little guy can do about it."

For all three items, an agree response was scored as powerlessness. Hulbary reports that his attitude scores were constructed by calculating factor scores from a principal component factor solution. The scores for his powerlessness scale are the standardized factor scores, and his scale ranged from -1.58 to $+1.71$. In presenting Hulbary's data I reversed the direction of his scores, so that high scores in Appendix A indicate *powerfulness* rather than powerlessness.

Political Trust Items developed by David O. Sears:[45]

1. "Do you think *policemen* can be trusted?"
2. "What do you think about *our government* . . . How often does it make mistakes?"
3. "How often do you think *the President* makes mistakes?"

Five-item Political Efficacy Scale developed by Edward G. Carmines:[46]

Carmines employed items 3, 4, 5, 6, and 7 used by Easton and Dennis. He performed interitem and item-total correlations with all five items. All the pairwise correlations were significant at the .001 level, and the correlations of the items with the total scale ranged from .54 to .70.

Four-item Political Efficacy Index developed by Samuel C. Funderburk:[47]

Funderburk used (with minor adaptations) items 4, 5, 6, and 7 employed by Easton and Dennis. He reports that intercorrelations between these items ranged from Pearson's *r*s of .34 to .46.

Four-item Political Trust Scale developed by Funderburk:[48]

Funderburk used items 2, 3, and 4 employed by Langton and Jennings, and added the following item:

1. "How much of the time do you think you can trust the city government to do what is right? a. just about all the time b. most of the time c. only some of the time d. hardly any of the time e. don't know, can't say."

Funderburk reports that these items were chosen on the basis of a factor analysis employing a principal component solution. He also reports that intercorrelations between these items ranged from Pearson' rs of .24 to .52.

Political Trust Item used by Dean Jaros and Kenneth L. Kolson:[49]

"How honest is the President? More honest than most · As honest as most   Less honest than most."

Three-item Political Cynicism Scale developed by Anthony M. Orum and Roberta S. Cohen:[50]

1. "Does the government make a lot of mistakes?"
2. "Can the government be trusted?"
3. "Are there some big powerful men running the government who do not care about us ordinary people?"

Orum and Cohen selected these items after conducting a principal component factor analysis with two 36-variable sets. The political cynicism scale had scores ranging from .64 to 2.56. In presenting their data I reversed the direction of their scores, so that high scores in Appendix A indicate political trust rather than political cynicism.

Five-item Political Cynicism Scale developed by Orum and Cohen:[51]

The five-item scale includes the three items above, plus the following two:

4. "Rich people are the ones who decide what goes on in government."
5. "The U.S. needs a complete change in its form of government."

Orum and Cohen selected these items after conducting a principal component factor analysis of two 36-variable sets. The five-item political cynicism scale had scores ranging from 1.54 to 6.16. In presenting their data I reversed the direction of their scores, so that high scores in Appendix A indicate political trust rather than political cynicism.

Eight-item Political Efficacy Scale developed by Christine Bennett Button:[52]

Button employed all eight efficacy items used by Easton and Dennis. She administered identical versions of her questionnaire two weeks apart to additional classrooms, which she did not include in her basic results. The political efficacy scale had a test-retest reliability of .845 (Pearson's r). She did not report procedures to test the unidimensionality of these items. Scores on this scale can range from a low of 8.0 to a high of 32.0.

Two-item Ability to Help Solve Local and National Problems Scale developed by Button:[53]

1. "What do you think are Austin's two biggest problems? Do you feel that you personally can do anything to help solve these problems?
       Yes No Don't know   If so, what? If no, why?"
2. "What do you think are America's two biggest problems? Do you feel that you personally can do anything to help solve these problems?
       Yes No Don't know   If so, what? If no, why?"

Button reports that this scale had a test-retest reliability of .640. She did not report procedures to test the unidimensionality of these items. Scores on this scale can range from a low of 2.0 to a high of 8.0.

Five-item Political Cynicism Scale developed by Button:[54]

Button employed items 2 through 6 used by Langton and Jennings (with a minor modification of item 6). She reports that this scale had a test-retest reliability of .522. She did not report procedures to test the unidimensionality of these items. Scores on this scale can range from a low of 5.0 to a high of 15.0. In presenting Button's data I reversed the direction of her scores, so that high scores in Appendix A indicate political trust rather than political cynicism.

Political Efficacy Items used by Richard C. Remy:[55]

1. "Sometimes politics and government seem so complicated that a person like me can't really understand what's going on.
Strongly agree   Agree   Don't know   Disagree   Strongly disagree."
2. "People like me don't have any say about what the government does."
3. "People like me can change what happens in the government."

For items 1 and 2 a disagree response was considered efficacious. For item 3, agreement was considered efficacious. In addition to these standard efficacy items, Remy's questionnaire employed eight items that measured efficacy toward foreign policy and world affairs.

Political Trust Items used by Remy:[56]

1. "I usually have confidence that the government will do what is right.
Agree   Disagree   Don't know."
2. "Most politicians don't seem to really mean what they say."
3. "When the going gets tough, the President can be trusted to level with the American people."
4. "Congress can't be trusted to represent the people fairly today."
5. "The Courts in this country can't be trusted to give a person a fair hearing."

Four-item Political Incapability Scale developed by Samuel Long:[57]

1. "I believe public officials don't care much what people like me and my parents think."
2. "There is no way other than voting that people like me and my parents can influence actions of the government."
3. "Sometimes politics and government seem so complicated that I can't really understand what's going on."
4. "People like me and my parents don't have any say about what the government does."

For all four items, agreement was scored as incapability. Long reports that this scale yielded a Cronbach's Alpha of .50. Scale scores ranged from 6.0 to 24.0. In presenting Long's data I reversed the direction of his scores, so that high scores in Appendix A indicate political *capability* rather than incapability.

Four-item Political Discontentment Scale developed by Long:[58]

1. "These days the government is trying to do too many things, including some activities that I don't think it has the right to do."
2. "For the most part, the government serves the interests of a few organized groups, such as business or labor, and isn't very concerned about the needs of people like my parents and me."
3. "It seems to me that the government often fails to take necessary actions on important matters, even when the people favor such action."
4. "As the government is now organized and operated, I think it is hopelessly incapable of dealing with all the crucial problems facing the country today."

For all four items, agreement was scored as discontent. Long reports that this scale yielded a Cronbach's Alpha of .61. Scale scores ranged from 6.0 to 24.0. In presenting Long's data I reversed the direction of his scores, so that high scores in Appendix A indicate political *contentment* rather than discontentment.

Political Trust Items used by Harold M. Barger in his 1973 questionnaire:[59]

1. "The President of the United States is very honest. Disagree very much   Disagree   No opinion   Agree   Agree very much."
2. "Police are very honest. Disagree very much   Disagree   No opinion   Agree   Agree very much."

Barger's 1974 questionnaire used the same items, but reduced the response range to Disagree, No opinion, and Agree.

Additional Political Efficacy Item used in the University of Michigan Survey Research Center's 1973 questionnaire:[60]

"I don't think public officials care much what people like me think."

Political Incapability Scale and Political Discontentment Scale used by Long in his May 1973 survey:[61]

Long used the same items reported above, but presented Kuder-Richardson reliability coefficients only for his combined political alienation measure that included both scales. Long presented his data in the form of z-scores. In presenting his data I reversed the direction of his scores, so that high scores in Appendix A indicate *capability* rather than incapability and political *contentment* rather than discontentment.

Two-item Political Efficacy Index used by Marjorie Randon Hershey:[62]

1. "There is nothing that people can do about government." (Disagreement scored as efficacious.)
2. "Americans have a chance to say what they think about running the government." (Agreement scored as efficacious.)

Three-item Political Trust Scale developed by Bruce A. Campbell:[63]

Campbell used items 3, 4, and 5 employed by Langton and Jennings. He reports that this scale was produced through a single-dimension principal component factor analysis. Scale scores ranged from 1.0 (high trust) to 5.0 (low trust). In presenting Campbell's data I reversed the direction of his scores, so that high scores in Appendix A indicate high political trust.

Political Efficacy Index used by Lorn S. Foster:[64]

Foster employed items 3, 4, 5, 6, and 7 used by Easton and Dennis (with a minor modification of item 5).

Political Trust Items used by Foster:[65]

1. "(Check one.) The President is *more honest* than most men. . . . The President is *as honest* as most men. . . . The President is *less honest* than most men."
2. "(Check one.) The mayor is *more honest* than most men. . . . The mayor is *as honest* as most men. . . . The mayor is *less honest* than most men."

Political Incapability Scale and Political Discontentment Scale developed by Long in his December 1974 survey:[66]

Long used the same items reported above. He reports that the Cronbach's Alpha reliability coefficient of the political incapability scale was .64, and that the reliability coefficient of the discontentment scale was .74. Long presented his data in the form of *z*-scores. In presenting his data I reversed the direction of his scores, so that high scores in Appendix A indicate political *capability* rather than incapability and *contentment* rather than discontentment.

Six-item Political Cynicism Scale developed by Long:[67]

1. "Money is the most important factor influencing public policies."
2. "Politicians represent the general interest more frequently than they represent special interests."
3. "In order to get nominated, most candidates for public office have to make basic compromises and undesirable commitments."
4. "Politicans spend most of their time getting re-elected or re-appointed."
5. "People are very frequently manipulated by politicans."
6. "A large number of city and county politicans are political hacks."

Except for item 2, agreement is scored as cynicism. Long reports that this scale had a Cronbach's Alpha reliability coefficient of .83. Long presented his data in the form of z-scores. In presenting his data I reversed the direction of his scores, so that high scores in Appendix A indicate political trust rather than political cynicism.

Political Incapability Scale, Political Discontentment Scale, and Political Cynicism Scale developed by Long in his May 1975 survey:[68]

Long used the same items reported above. He reports that the Cronbach's Alpha coefficients of these scales were .49, .58, and .50, respectively. The political incapability and discontentment scales ranged from 6 through 24, the political cynicism scale from 6 through 36. The scores presented in Appendix A are reflected so that high scores indicate political *capability* rather than incapability, *contentment* rather than discontentment, and *trust* rather than cynicism.

NOTES

1. David Easton and Jack Dennis, "The Child's Acquisition of Regime Norms: Political Efficacy," *American Political Science Review*, 61 (March 1967), pp. 25–38, at pp. 29–31. The complete questionnaire is reproduced in Robert D. Hess and Judith V. Torney, *The Development of Basic Attitudes and Values Toward Government and Citizenship During the Elementary School*

Years, Part 1, Report to U.S. Office of Education on Cooperative Project No. 1078 (Chicago: University of Chicago, 1965), pp. 473–492.

2. Kenneth P. Langton and M. Kent Jennings, "Political Socialization and the High School Civics Curriculum in the United States," *American Political Science Review,* 62 (September 1968), pp. 852–867, at p. 856.

3. See M. Kent Jennings and Richard G. Niemi, *The Political Character of Adolescence: The Influence of Families and Schools* (Princeton, N.J.: Princeton University Press, 1974), p. 141.

4. James T. Jones, "Political Socialization in a Mid-Western Industrial Community," unpublished Ph.D. dissertation, University of Illinois, 1965, p. 167.

5. Based directly upon the University of Michigan Survey Research Center (SRC) questionnaire for the National Study of High School Seniors.

6. Based directly upon the University of Michigan SRC questionnaire.

7. Langton and Jennings, "Political Socialization and the High School Curriculum," p. 856.

8. Jerald G. Bachman, *Youth in Transition, Volume 2: The Impact of Family Background and Intelligence on Tenth Grade Boys* (Ann Arbor, Mich.: Institute for Social Research, 1970), pp. 150–152.

9. Henry I. Penfield, Jr., "The Political Socialization of the Alabama School Child," unpublished Ph.D. dissertation, University of Alabama, pp. 207–208.

10. *Ibid.,* pp. 203–205.

11. Lee H. Ehman, "Political Socialization and the High School Social Studies Curriculum," unpublished Ph.D. dissertation, University of Michigan, 1969, pp. 50–51. See also Ehman, "Political Efficacy and the High School Social Studies Curriculum," in *Political Youth, Traditional Schools: National and International Perspectives,* ed. Byron G. Massialas (Englewood Cliffs, N.J.: Prentice-Hall, 1972), pp. 90–102, at p. 93.

12. Ehman, "Political Socialization and the High School Social Studies Curriculum," pp. 51–52.

13. Sandra J. Kenyon, "The Development of Political Cynicism among Negro and White Adolescents," paper presented at 65th Annual Meeting of American Political Science Association, New York, September 1969, note 20.

14. *Ibid.,* note 11. See also Sandra Kenyon Schwartz, "Patterns of Cynicism: Differential Political Socialization among Adolescents," in *New Directions in Political Socialization,* eds. David C. Schwartz and Sandra Kenyon Schwartz (New York: Free Press, 1975), pp. 188–202, at p. 191.

15. Jack Dennis, *Political Learning in Childhood and Adolescence: A Study of Fifth, Eighth, and Eleventh Graders in Milwaukee, Wisconsin* (Madison: Wisconsin Research and Development Center for Cognitive Learning, 1969), p. 25.

16. *Ibid.*

17. *Ibid.,* p. 24.

18. Jack K. Masson, "Political Socialization Study of Seattle Children," unpublished Ph.D. dissertation, University of Washington, 1971, p. 203.

19. *Ibid.,* p. 204.

20. Joan E. Laurence, "White Socialization: Black Reality," *Psychiatry,* 33 (May 1970), pp. 174–194, at p. 179.

21. Edward S. Greenberg, "Political Socialization to Support of the System: A Comparison of Black and White Children," unpublished Ph.D. dissertation, University of Wisconsin, 1969, pp. 270, 274.

22. Thomas J. Williams, "Subcultural Differences in Political Socialization among Selected Children in Georgia," unpublished Ph.D. dissertation, University of Georgia, 1972, pp. 354–355.

23. *Ibid.,* pp. 348, 353.

24. Based directly upon Krause's questionnaire. For the scoring procedures, see Merton S. Krause, "Schoolchildren's Attitudes Toward Public Authority Figures," Institute for Juvenile Reasearch, Chicago, August 1972, mimeo, p. 3. See also Krause, "Schoolchildren's Attitudes Toward Public Authority Figures," *Adolescence,* 10 (Spring 1975), pp. 111–122, at pp. 113–114. Krause's more recent paper does not report differences according to race.

25. Based directly upon Krause's questionnaire.

26. *Ibid.*

27. *Ibid.*

28. *Ibid.*

29. *Ibid.*

30. Alden J. Stevens, "Children's Acquisition of Regime Norms in Subcultures of Race and Social Class: The Problem of System Maintenance," unpublished Ph.D. dissertation, University of Maryland, 1969, pp. 45–46, 122–123.

31. Schley R. Lyons, "The Political Socialization of Ghetto Children: Efficacy and Cynicism," *Journal of Politics,* 32 (May 1970), pp. 288–304, at pp. 290–291.

32. *Ibid.,* pp. 291–292.

33. Pauline Marie Vaillancourt, "The Political Socialization of Young People: A Panel Survey of Youngsters in the San Francisco Bay Area," unpublished Ph.D. dissertation, University of California at Berkeley, 1972, pp. 70–71, 384–385.

34. *Ibid.,* pp. 382–383.

35. Anne M. Heinz, "Black Pride as a System-Transforming Variable: Its Impact on Self-Image and Attitudes Toward Authority," unpublished Ph.D. dissertation, Northwestern University, 1971, pp. 90–91, 196. Heinz refers to the first two items as measures of political efficacy but, given our formulation, they measure components of political trust, the belief that political leaders are competent and that they act in the interests of the people.

36. Sarah F. Liebschutz and Richard G. Niemi, "Political Attitudes among Black Children," in *The Politics of Future Citizens: New Directions in the Political Socialization of Children,* ed. Richard G. Niemi (San Francisco: Jossey-Bass, 1974), pp. 83–102, at pp. 90–91.

37. Harrell R. Rodgers, Jr., "Toward Explanation of the Political Efficacy

and Political Cynicism of Black Adolescents: An Exploratory Study," *American Journal of Political Science,* 18 (May 1974), pp. 257–282, at pp. 261–262.

38. *Ibid.*

39. Harrell R. Rodgers, Jr., and Edward B. Lewis, "Political Support and Compliance Attitudes: A Study of Adolescents," *American Politics Quarterly,* 2 (January 1974), pp. 61–77, at p. 76.

40. Harrell R. Rodgers, Jr., and George Taylor, "The Policeman as an Agent of Regime Legitimation," *Midwest Journal of Political Science,* 15 (February 1971), pp. 72–86, at pp. 75–76.

41. *Ibid.,* p. 80.

42. George H. Strauss, "The Protest Generation: Political Disenchantment and Activism among American High School Students," unpublished Ph.D. dissertation, New York University, 1973, pp. 131–132; p. 10 of questionnaire.

43. *Ibid.,* pp. 144–145; p. 10 of questionnaire.

44. William E. Hulbary, "Adolescent Political Self-Images and Political Involvement: The Relative Effects of High School Black Studies Courses and Prior Socialization," unpublished Ph.D. dissertation, University of Iowa, 1972, pp. 40–47; and Hulbary, "Information Redundancy and High School Black Studies Courses: A Research Note," *Education and Urban Society,* 7 (November 1974), pp. 96–109, at pp. 100–102, 108.

45. David O. Sears, "Political Socialization," in *Handbook of Political Science, Volume 2: Micropolitical Theory,* eds. Fred I. Greenstein and Nelson W. Polsby (Reading, Mass.: Addison-Wesley, 1975), pp. 93–153, at p. 109.

46. Edward G. Carmines, "Race, Intelligence, and Sense of Political Efficacy: A Multivariate Political Socialization Study," unpublished M.A. thesis, College of William and Mary, 1972, pp. 57–59.

47. Samuel C. Funderburk, "Orientations Toward Protest and Violence among Children and Adolescents," unpublished Ph.D. dissertation, University of Iowa, 1973, pp. 54–55, 136–137.

48. *Ibid.,* pp. 46–48, 131.

49. Dean Jaros and Kenneth L. Kolson, "The Multifarious Leader: Political Socialization of Amish, 'Yanks,' Blacks," in *The Politics of Future Citizens: New Dimensions in the Political Socialization of Children,* ed. Richard G. Niemi (San Francisco: Jossey-Bass, 1974), pp. 41–62, at p. 54.

50. Anthony M. Orum and Roberta S. Cohen, "The Development of Political Orientations among Black and White Children," *American Sociological Review,* 38 (February 1973), pp. 62–74, at p. 64.

51. *Ibid.,* pp. 64–65.

52. Christine Bennett Button, "The Development of Experimental Curriculum to Effect the Political Socialization of Anglo, Black and Mexican-American Adolescents," unpublished Ph.D. dissertation, University of Texas, 1972, pp. 21–24. See also Button, "Political Education for Minority Groups," in *The Politics of Future Citizens: New Dimensions in the Political Socialization of Children,* ed. Richard G. Niemi (San Francisco: Jossey-Bass, 1974), pp. 167–198, at pp. 174–175.

53. Button, "The Development of Experimental Curriculum," p. 24; Button, "Political Education for Minority Groups," p. 175.

54. Button, "The Development of Experimental Curriculum," pp. 20–21; Button, "Political Education for Minority Groups," pp. 173–174.

55. Based directly upon Remy's questionnaire.

56. *Ibid.*

57. Samuel Long, "Malevolent Estrangement: Political Alienation and Political [Violence] Justification among Black and White Adolescents," *Youth and Society,* 7 (December 1975), pp. 99–129, at p. 124. Information about the range of scale scores was provided by a personal communication.

58. *Ibid.* Information about the range of scale scores was provided by a personal communication.

59. Based directly upon Barger's questionnaire.

60. Based directly upon the University of Michigan Survey Research Center questionnaire for their National Study of High School Seniors.

61. Samuel Long, "Socialization to Revolt: Political Alienation and Political Violence Condonation among White and Black Youth," paper presented at 70th Annual Meeting of American Political Science Association, Chicago, August-September 1974, note 47.

62. Provided by a personal communication.

63. The data in Appendix A are based upon a personal communication. However, the political trust scale is described in Bruce A. Campbell, "The Acquisition of Political Trust: Explorations of Socialization Theory," paper presented at 71st Annual Meeting of American Political Science Association, San Francisco, September 1975, p. 8; note 11.

64. Based directly upon Foster's questionnaire.

65. *Ibid.*

66. Samuel Long, "Political Alienation among Black and White Adolescents: A Test of the Social Deprivation and Political Reality Models, *American Politics Quarterly,* 4 (July 1976), pp. 267–303, at p. 296.

67. *Ibid.*

68. The data in Appendix A are based upon a personal communication. However the scales are described in Samuel Long, "Cognitive-Perceptual Factors in the Political Alienation Process: A Test of Six Models," paper presented at 34th Annual Meeting of Midwest Political Science Association, Chicago, April-May 1976, at pp. 12–13. The information about the range of scores for the scales was also provided in a personal communication.

APPENDIX D

Basic Assumptions and Empirical Consequences of the Four Explanations

POLITICAL-EDUCATION EXPLANATION

A. Racial differences (in feelings of political efficacy and trust) result from differences in political education within American schools—the *political-education* explanation.

Assumption A.1. Students learn the political values taught in the schools. In other words, the schools are effective agents of political socialization.

Assumption A.2. Teachers are less likely to stress norms of political participation when teaching black children than when teaching white children.

Empirical Consequence A.1. Black children should be less likely to have a participatory view of the polity and their role within the polity than white children have.

SOCIAL-DEPRIVATION EXPLANATION

B. Racial differences result from social-structural conditions that contribute to low feelings of self-confidence among blacks—the *social-deprivation* explanation.

Assumption B.1. Persons deprived of opportunity and denied respect tend to have low levels of self-confidence and, in particular, a feeling that they cannot control their social environment.

Assumption B.2. Persons who have low levels of self-confidence tend to have low feelings of political effectiveness.

Assumption B.3. Persons who have low levels of self-confidence tend to have low feelings of political trust.

Assumption B.4. Black children are deprived of opportunity and denied respect.

Assumption B.5. Black children have lower levels of self-confidence than white children have and, in particular, are less likely to feel they can control their social environment.

Empirical Consequence B.1. In social settings where blacks have higher levels of social opportunity, they should have higher feelings of political effectiveness and political trust. Controlling for social opportunity should reduce or eliminate differences in political attitudes.

Empirical Consequence B.2. Black children with high feelings of self-confidence should be more politically efficacious and more trusting than those with low feelings of self-confidence. Controlling for feelings of self-confidence should reduce or eliminate racial differences in political attitudes.

Assumptions of the "Simplified" Social-Deprivation Explanation

New Assumption B.1. Persons who are socially deprived tend to conclude they are politically powerless.

New Assumption B.2. Persons who are socially deprived tend to resent political authorities and conclude they cannot be trusted.

New Assumption B.3. Black children are deprived of opportunity and denied respect.

INTELLIGENCE EXPLANATION

C. Racial differences result from differences in intelligence—the *intelligence* explanation.

Assumption C.1. Low levels of intelligence contribute to low feelings of political effectiveness.

Assumption C.2. Blacks tend to be less intelligent than whites.

Empirical Consequence C.1. Among black children, those with high intelligence scores should feel more politically efficacious than those with low intelligence scores. Controlling for intelligence should reduce or eliminate racial differences in sense of political effectiveness.

POLITICAL-REALITY EXPLANATION

D. Racial differences result from differences in the political environment in which blacks and whites live—the *political-reality* explanation.

Assumption D.1. Blacks have less capacity to influence political leaders than whites have.

Assumption D.2. Political leaders are less trustworthy in their dealings with blacks than in their dealings with whites.

Assumption D.3. Black children know these facts, or they are indirectly influenced by adults who know these facts, or both.

Empirical Consequence D.1. Feelings of political effectiveness and political trust should be lower among blacks who understand political realities than among those who do not.

Empirical Consequence D.2. Racial differences in feelings of political efficacy should be reduced or reversed in settings where blacks have political power.

Empirical Consequence D.3. Blacks should be more trusting toward political leaders who depend upon black electoral support than toward leaders who do not rely on black support.

Bibliography

Part 1 Studies Reporting Feelings of Political Efficacy and Political Trust among Black and White Schoolchildren

Bachman, Jerald G. *Youth in Transition, Volume 2: The Impact of Family Background and Intelligence on Tenth-Grade Boys.* Ann Arbor, Mich.: Institute for Social Research, 1970.

Barger, Harold M. "Images of the President and Policemen among Black, Mexican-American and Anglo School Children: Considerations on Watergate." Paper presented at 70th Annual Meeting of American Political Science Association, Chicago, August-September 1974.

Button, Christine Bennett. "The Development of Experimental Curriculum to Effect the Political Socialization of Anglo, Black, and Mexican-American Adolescents." Unpublished Ph.D. dissertation, University of Texas, 1972.

————. "Political Education for Minority Groups," in Richard G. Niemi (ed.), *The Politics of Future Citizens: New Dimensions in the Political Socialization of Children.* San Francisco: Jossey-Bass, 1974, pp. 167–198.

Carmines, Edward G. "Race, Intelligence and Sense of Political Efficacy: A Multivariate Political Socialization Study." Unpublished M.A. thesis, College of William and Mary, 1972.

Dennis, Jack. *Political Learning in Childhood and Adolescence: A Study of Fifth, Eighth, and Eleventh Graders in Milwaukee, Wisconsin.* Madison: Wisconsin Research and Development Center for Cognitive Learning, 1969.

Ehman, Lee H. "Political Efficacy and the High School Social Studies Curriculum," in Byron G. Massialas (ed.), *Political Youth, Traditional Schools: National and International Perspectives.* Englewood Cliffs, N.J.: Prentice-Hall, 1972, pp. 90–102.

————. "Political Socialization and the High School Social Studies Curriculum." Unpublished Ph.D. dissertation, University of Michigan, 1969.

Foster, Lorn S. "Children's Attitudes Toward Political Participation: A Comparative Study," unpublished Ph.D. dissertation, University of Illinois, 1976.

Funderburk, Samuel C. "Orientations Toward Protest and Violence among Children and Adolescents." Unpublished Ph.D. dissertation, University of Iowa, 1973.

Greenberg, Edward S. "Political Socialization to Support of the System: A Comparison of Black and White Children." Unpublished Ph.D. dissertation, University of Wisconsin, 1969.

Heinz, Anne M. "Black Pride as a System-Transforming Variable: Its Impact on Self-Image and Attitudes Toward Authority." Unpublished Ph.D. dissertation, Northwestern University, 1971.

Hulbary, William E. "Adolescent Political Self-Images and Political Involvement: The Relative Effects of High School Black Studies Courses and Prior Socialization." Unpublished Ph.D. dissertation, University of Iowa, 1972.

————. "Information Redundancy and High School Black Courses: A Research Note." *Education and Urban Society,* 7 (November 1974), pp. 96–109.

Jaros, Dean, and Kolson, Kenneth L. "The Multifarious Leader: Political Socialization of Amish, 'Yanks,' Blacks," in Richard G. Niemi (ed.), *The Politics of Future Citizens: New Dimensions in the Political Socialization of Children.* San Francisco: Jossey-Bass, 1974, pp. 41–62.

Jennings, M. Kent, and Niemi, Richard G. *The Political Character of Adolescence: The Influence of Families and Schools.* Princeton, N.J.: Princeton University Press, 1974.

Jones, James T. "Political Socialization in a Mid-Western Industrial Community." Unpublished Ph.D. dissertation, University of Illinois, 1965.

Kenyon, Sandra J. "The Development of Political Cynicism among Negro and White Adolescents." Paper presented at 65th Annual Meeting of American Political Science Association, New York, September 1969.

————. "The Development of Political Cynicism: A Study of Political Socialization." Unpublished Ph.D. dissertation, Massachusetts Institute of Technology, 1970.

Krause, Merton S. "Schoolchildren's Attitudes Toward Public Authority Figures." Institute for Juvenile Research, Chicago, August 1972, mimeo.

Langton, Kenneth P., and Jennings, M. Kent. "Political Socialization and the High School Civics Curriculum in the United States." *American Political Science Review,* 62 (September 1968), pp. 852–867.

Laurence, Joan E. "White Socialization: Black Reality." *Psychiatry,* 33 (May 1970), pp. 174–194.

Liebschutz, Sarah F., and Niemi, Richard G. "Political Attitudes among Black Children," in Richard G. Niemi (ed.), *The Politics of Future Citizens: New Dimensions in the Political Socialization of Children.* (San Francisco: Jossey-Bass, 1974, pp. 83–102.

Long, Samuel. "Malevolent Estrangement: Political Alienation and Political Violence Justification among Black and White Adolescents." Paper presented at 32d Annual Meeting of Midwest Political Science Association, Chicago, April 1974.

——. "Malevolent Estrangement: Political Alienation and Political [Violence] Justification among Black and White Adolescents." *Youth and Society,* 7 (December 1975), pp. 99–129.

——. "Political Alienation among Black and White Adolescents: A Test of the Social Deprivation and Political Reality Models." *American Politics Quarterly,* 4 (July 1976), pp. 267–303.

——. "Socialization to Revolt: Political Alienation and Political Violence Condonation among White and Black Youth." Paper presented at 70th Annual Meeting of American Political Science Association, Chicago, August-September 1974.

——. "Sociopolitical Antecedents of Political Alienation among Black and White Adolescents: Social Deprivation and/or Political Reality?" Paper presented at 70th Annual Meeting of American Sociological Association, San Francisco, August 1975.

——. "Sociopolitical Reality and Political Alienation: A Comparison of White and Black Adolescents." Paper presented at 29th Annual Meeting of Western Political Science Association, Seattle, March 1975.

Lyons, Schley R. "The Political Socialization of Ghetto Children: Efficacy and Cynicism." *Journal of Politics,* 32 (May 1970), pp. 288–304.

Masson, Jack K. "Political Socialization Study of Seattle Children." Unpublished Ph.D. dissertation, University of Washington, 1971.

Orum, Anthony M., and Cohen, Roberta S. "The Development of Political Orientations among Black and White Children." *American Sociological Review,* 38 (February 1973), pp. 62–74.

Penfield, Henry I., Jr. "The Political Socialization of the Alabama School Child." Unpublished Ph.D. dissertation, University of Alabama, 1970.

Rodgers, Harrell R., Jr. "Toward Explanation of the Political Efficacy and Political Cynicism of Black Adolescents: An Exploratory Study." *American Journal of Political Science,* 18 (May 1974), pp. 257–282.

——. "Toward Explanation of the Political Efficacy and Political Cynicism of Black Schoolchildren." Paper presented at Annual Meeting of Southwestern Social Science Association, San Antonio, March-April 1972.

——, and Lewis, Edward B. "Political Support and Compliance Attitudes: A Study of Adolescents." *American Politics Quarterly,* 2 (January 1974), pp. 61–77.

——, and Taylor, George. "The Policeman as an Agent of Regime Legitimation." *Midwest Journal of Political Science,* 15 (February 1971), pp. 72–86.

Sears, David O. "Political Socialization," in Fred I. Greenstein and Nelson W. Polsby (eds.), *Handbook of Political Science, Volume 2: Micropolitical Theory.* Reading, Mass.: Addison-Wesley, 1975, pp. 93–153.

Stevens, Alden J. "Children's Acquisition of Regime Norms in Subcultures of Race and Social Class: The Problem of System Maintenance." Unpublished Ph.D. dissertation, University of Maryland, 1969.

Strauss, George H. "The Protest Generation: Political Disenchantment and Activism among American High School Students." Unpublished Ph.D. dissertation, New York University, 1973.

Vaillancourt, Pauline Marie. "The Political Socialization of Young People: A Panel Survey of Youngsters in the San Francisco Bay Area." Unpublished Ph.D. dissertation, University of California at Berkeley, 1972.

Williams, Thomas J. "Racial Differences in Southern Children's Attitudes Toward Presidential Authority." *Georgia Political Science Association Journal,* 2 (Spring 1974), pp. 89–121.

——. "Subcultural Differences in Political Socialization among Selected Children in Georgia." Unpublished Ph.D. dissertation, University of Georgia, 1972.

Part 2   Other Sources Cited

Aberbach, Joel D., and Walker, Jack L. *Race in the City: Political Trust and Public Policy in the New Urban System.* Boston: Little, Brown, 1973.

Abramson, Paul R. *Generational Change in American Politics.* Lexington, Mass.: Heath, 1975.

———. "Political Efficacy and Political Trust among Black Schoolchildren: Four Alternative Explanations." Paper presented at Conference on Political Theory and Political Education, Michigan State University, February 1971.

———. "Political Efficacy and Political Trust among Black Schoolchildren: Four Explanations." Revised version of paper presented at Conference on Political Theory and Political Education, Michigan State University. (Revised paper dated May 1971.)

———. "Political Efficacy and Political Trust among Black Schoolchildren: Two Explanations." *Journal of Politics,* 34 (November 1972), pp. 1243–1275.

———, and Inglehart, Ronald. "The Development of Systemic Support in Four Western Democracies." *Comparative Political Studies,* 2 (January 1970), pp. 419–442.

Agger, Robert E.; Goldstein, Marshall N.; and Pearl, Stanley A. "Political Cynicism: Measurement and Meaning." *Journal of Politics,* 23 (August 1961), pp. 477–506.

Almond, Gabriel A., and Verba, Sidney, *The Civic Culture: Political Attitudes and Democracy in Five Nations.* Princeton, N.J.: Princeton University Press, 1963.

Asher, Herbert B. "The Reliability of the Political Efficacy Items." *Political Methodology,* 1 (Spring 1974), pp. 45–72.

Axelrod, Robert. "Communication." *American Political Science Review,* 68 (June 1974), pp. 717–720.

———, "Where the Votes Come From: An Analysis of Electoral Coalitions, 1952–1968." *American Political Science Review,* 66 (March 1972), pp. 11–20.

Babbie, Earl R. *Survey Research Methods.* Belmont, Calif.: Wadsworth, 1973.

Balch, George I. "Multiple Indicators in Survey Research: The Concept 'Sense of Political Efficacy.'" *Political Methodology,* 1 (Spring 1974), pp. 1–43.

Barker, Lucius J., and McCorry, Jesse J., Jr. *Black Americans and the Political System.* Cambridge, Mass.: Winthrop, 1976.

Baughman, E. Earl. *Black Americans: A Psychological Analysis.* New York: Academic Press, 1971.

———, and Dahlstrom, W. Grant. *Negro and White Children: A Psychological Study in the Rural South.* New York: Academic Press, 1968.

Billings, Charles E. "Black Activists and the Schools." *The High School Journal,* 54 (November 1970), pp. 96–107.

Blau, Peter M., and Duncan, Otis Dudley. *The American Occupational Structure.* New York: Wiley, 1967.

Bodmer, W. F. "Race and IQ: The Genetic Background," in Ken Richardson and David Spears (eds.), *Race, Culture and Intelligence.* Harmondsworth, Middlesex: Penguin, 1972, pp. 83–113.

Campbell, Angus; Converse, Philip E.; Miller, Warren E.; and Stokes, Donald E. *The American Voter.* New York: Wiley, 1960.

———; Gurin, Gerald; and Miller, Warren E. *The Voter Decides.* Evanston, Ill.: Row, Peterson, 1954.

Campbell, Bruce A. "The Acquisition of Political Trust: Explorations of Socialization Theory." Paper presented at 71st Annual Meeting of American Political Science Association, San Francisco, September 1975.

———. "Racial Differences in the Reaction to Watergate: Some Implications for Political Support." *Youth and Society,* 7 (June 1976), pp. 439–459.

Canady, Herman G. "The Effect of 'Rapport' on the I.Q.: A New Approach to the Problem of Racial Psychology." *Journal of Negro Education,* 5 (April 1936), pp. 209–219.

Caplan, Nathan. "The New Ghetto Man: A Review of Recent Empirical Studies." *Journal of Social Issues,* 26 (Winter 1970), pp. 59–73.

Citrin, Jack. "Comment: The Political Relevance of Trust in Government." *American Political Science Review,* 68 (September 1974), pp. 973–988.

———. *Political Disaffection in America.* Englewood Cliffs, N.J.: Prentice-Hall, forthcoming.

———; McClosky, Herbert; Shanks, J. Merrill; and Sniderman, Paul M. "Personal and Political Sources of Political Alienation." *British Journal of Political Science,* 5 (January 1975), pp. 1–31.

Clark, Kenneth B. *Dark Ghetto: Dilemmas of Social Power.* New York: Harper and Row, 1965.

———, and Clark, Mamie K. "The Development of Consciousness of Self and the Emergence of Racial Identification in Negro Preschool Children." *Journal of Social Psychology,* 10 (November 1939), pp. 591–599.

Clarke, James W. "Family Structure and Political Socialization among Urban Black Children." *American Journal of Political Science,* 17 (May 1973), pp. 302–315.

Cole, Richard L. "Toward a Model of Political Trust: A Causal Analysis." *American Journal of Political Science,* 17 (November 1973), pp. 809–817.

Coleman, James S. et al. *Equality of Educational Opportunity.* Washington, D.C.: U.S. Government Printing Office, 1966.

Converse, Philip E. "Change in the American Electorate," in Angus Campbell and Philip E. Converse (eds.), *The Human Meaning of Social Change.* New York: Russell Sage, 1972, pp. 263–337.

Cronbach, Lee J. "Heredity, Environment, and Educational Policy." *Harvard Educational Review,* 39 (Spring 1969), pp. 338–347.

Dahl, Robert A. *A Preface to Democratic Theory.* Chicago: University of Chicago Press, 1956.

Douvan, Elizabeth, and Walker, Alan M. "The Sense of Effectiveness in Public Affairs." *Psychological Monographs: General and Applied,* 70 (Whole No. 429), 1956.

Dowse, Robert E., and Hughes, John. "The Family, The School, and the Political Socialization Process." *Sociology,* 5 (January 1971), pp. 21–45.

Easton, David. "A Re-Assessment of the Concept of Political Support." *British Journal of Political Science,* 5 (October 1975), pp. 435–457.

———. *A Systems Analysis of Political Life.* New York: Wiley, 1965.

———, and Dennis, Jack. *Children in the Political System: Origins of Political Legitimacy.* New York: McGraw-Hill, 1969.

———. "The Child's Acquisition of Regime Norms: Political Efficacy." *American Political Science Review,* 61 (March 1967), pp. 25–38.

Ehman, Lee H., and Gillespie, Judith A. "Political Life in the Hidden Curriculum: Does It Make a Difference?" Paper presented at 54th Annual Meeting of National Council for the Social Studies, Chicago, November 1974.

Ellis, Albert. *Reason and Emotion in Psychotherapy.* New York: Lyle Stuart, 1962.

Engstrom, Richard L. "Race and Compliance: Differential Political Socialization." *Polity,* 3 (Fall 1970), pp. 100–111.

Erikson, Erik H. *Childhood and Society.* 2d ed. New York: Norton, 1963.

Eysenck, Hans J. *The IQ Argument: Race, Intelligence and Education.* New York: Library Press, 1971.

Farris, Charles D. "Selected Attitudes on Foreign Affairs as Correlates of Authoritarianism and Political Anomie." *Journal of Politics,* 22 (February 1960), pp. 50–67.

Finifter, Ada W. "Concepts of Alienation, Introduction," in Ada W. Finifter (ed.), *Alienation and the Social System.* New York: Wiley, 1972, pp. 3–11.

———. "Dimensions of Political Alienation." *American Political Science Review,* 64 (June 1970), pp. 389–410.

———, and Abramson, Paul R. "City Size and Feelings of Political Competence." *Public Opinion Quarterly,* 39 (Summer 1975), pp. 189–198.

Form, William H., and Huber, Joan. "Income, Race, and the Ideology of Political Efficacy." *Journal of Politics,* 33 (August 1971), pp. 659–688.

Forward, John R., and Williams, Jay R. "Internal-External Control and Black Militancy." *Journal of Social Issues,* 26 (Winter 1970), pp. 75–92.

Gamson, William A. *Power and Discontent.* Homewood, Ill.: Dorsey, 1968.

Gough, Harrison G. "A Nonintellectual Intelligence Test." *Journal of Consulting Psychology,* 17 (August 1953), pp. 242–246.

Greenberg, Edward S. "Black Children and the Political System." *Public Opinion Quarterly,* 34 (Fall 1970), pp. 333–345.

––––––. "Black Children, Self-Esteem and the Liberation Movement." *Politics and Society,* 2 (Spring 1972), pp. 293–307.

––––––. "Children and Government: A Comparison Across Racial Lines." *Midwest Journal of Political Science,* 14 (May 1970), pp. 249–275.

Greenstein, Fred I. "The Benevolent Leader Revisited: Children's Images of Political Leaders in Three Democracies." *American Political Science Review,* 69 (December 1975), pp. 1371–1398.

––––––. "Personality and Politics," in Fred I. Greenstein and Nelson W. Polsby (eds.), *Handbook of Political Science, Volume 2: Micropolitical Theory.* Reading, Mass.: Addison-Wesley, 1975, pp. 1–92.

––––––. "The Standing of Social and Psychological Variables: An Addendum to Jackman's Critique." *Journal of Politics,* 32 (November 1970), pp. 989–992.

Grier, William H., and Cobbs, Price M. *Black Rage.* New York: Basic Books, 1968.

Grotelueschen, Thomas S. "The Political Orientations of Black Children in Northern Florida." Unpublished Ph.D. dissertation, University of Wisconsin, 1973.

Grove, D. John; Remy, Richard C.; and Zeigler, L. Harmon. "The Effects of Political Ideology and Educational Climates on Student Dissent." *American Politics Quarterly,* 2 (July 1974), pp. 259–275.

Gurin, Patricia; Gurin, Gerald; Lao, Rosina C.; and Beattie, Muriel. "Internal-External Control in the Motivational Dynamics of Negro Youth." *Journal of Social Issues,* 25 (Summer 1969), pp. 29–53.

Haggstrom, Warren C. "The Power of the Poor," in Frank Riessman, Jerome Cohen, and Arthur Pearl (eds.), *Mental Health of the Poor: New Treatment Approaches for Low Income People.* New York: Free Press, 1964, pp. 205–223.

Harvey, S.K., and Harvey, T. G. "Adolescent Political Outlooks: The Effects of Intelligence as an Independent Variable." *Midwest Journal of Political Science,* 14 (November 1970), pp. 565–595.

Hershey, Marjorie Randon, and Hill, David B. "Watergate and Preadults' Attitudes Toward the President." *American Journal of Political Science,* 19 (November 1975), pp. 703–726.

Hess, Robert D., and Torney, Judith V. *The Development of Basic Attitudes and Values Toward Government and Citizenship During the Elementary School Years, Part I.* Report to U.S. Office of Education on Cooperative Project No. 1078. Chicago: University of Chicago, 1965.

––––––. *The Development of Political Attitudes in Children.* Chicago: Aldine, 1967.

House, James S., and Mason, William M. "Political Alienation in America, 1952–1968." *American Sociological Review,* 40 (April 1975), pp. 123–147.

Hyman, Herbert H. "Dimensions of Social-Psychological Change in the Negro Population," in Angus Campbell and Philip E. Converse (eds.), *The Human Meaning of Social Change.* New York: Russell Sage, 1972, pp. 339–390.

Inkeles, Alex. "Social Structure and the Socialization of Competence." *Harvard Educational Review,* 36 (Summer 1966), pp. 265–283.

Jackman, Robert W. "A Note on Intelligence, Social Class, and Political Efficacy in Children." *Journal of Politics,* 32 (November 1970), pp. 984–989.

Jacob, Herbert. "Problems of Scale Equivalency in Measuring Attitudes in American Subcultures." *Social Science Quarterly,* 52 (June 1971), pp. 61–75.

Jaros, Dean. "Children's Orientations Toward Political Authority: A Detroit Study." Unpublished Ph.D. dissertation, Vanderbilt University, 1966.

———. "Children's Orientations Toward the President: Some Additional Theoretical Considerations and Data." *Journal of Politics,* 29 (May 1967), pp. 368–387.

———. *Socialization to Politics.* New York: Praeger, 1973.

———; Hirsch, Herbert; and Fleron, Frederic J., Jr. "The Malevolent Leader: Political Socialization in an American Sub-culture." *American Political Science Review,* 62 (June 1968), pp. 564–575.

Jencks, Christopher S. "The Coleman Report and Conventional Wisdom," in Frederick Mosteller and Daniel P. Moynihan (eds.), *On Equality of Educational Opportunity.* New York: Vintage Books, 1972, pp. 69–115.

Jennings, M. Kent, and Niemi, Richard G. "The Transmission of Political Values from Parent to Child." *American Political Science Review,* 62 (March 1968), pp. 169–184.

Jensen, Arthur R. *Educability and Group Differences.* New York: Harper and Row, 1973.

———. "How Much Can We Boost IQ and Scholastic Achievement?" *Harvard Educational Review,* 39 (Winter 1969), pp. 1–123.

Joe, Victor Clark. "Review of the Internal-External Control Construct as a Personality Variable." *Psychological Reports,* 28 (1971), pp. 619–640.

Kardiner, Abram, and Ovesey, Lionel. *The Mark of Oppression: Explorations in the Personality of the American Negro.* Cleveland: World, 1951.

Klineberg, Otto. *Negro Intelligence and Selective Migration.* New York: Columbia University Press, 1935.

Knowles, Louis L., and Prewitt, Kenneth (eds.). *Institutional Racism in America.* Englewood Cliffs, N.J.: Prentice-Hall, 1969.

Kornhauser, Arthur; Sheppard, Harold L.; and Mayer, Albert J. *When Labor Votes: A Study of Auto Workers.* New York: University Books, 1956.

Kozol, Jonathan. *Death at an Early Age: The Destruction of the Hearts and Minds of Negro Children in the Boston Public Schools.* New York: Bantam Books, 1967.

Krause, Merton S. "Schoolchildren's Attitudes Toward Public Authority Figures." *Adolescence,* 10 (Spring 1975), pp. 111–122.

Lane, Robert E. *Political Life: Why and How People Get Involved in Politics.* Glencoe, Ill.: Free Press, 1959.

Langton, Kenneth P., and Karns, David A. "The Relative Influence of the Family, Peer Group, and School in the Development of Political Efficacy." *Western Political Quarterly,* 21 (December 1969), pp. 813–826.

Layzer, David. "Heritability Analyses of IQ Scores: Science or Numerology?" *Science,* 183 (29 March 1974), pp. 1259–1266.

Leacock, Eleanor Burke. *Teaching and Learning in City Schools: A Comparative Study.* New York: Basic Books, 1969.

Levin, Martin L. "Social Climates and Political Socialization." *Public Opinion Quarterly,* 25 (Winter 1961), pp. 596–606.

Levitan, Sar A.; Johnston, William B.; and Taggart, Robert. *Still a Dream: The Changing Status of Blacks Since 1960.* Cambridge, Mass.: Harvard University Press, 1975.

Lewontin, Richard C. "Race and Intelligence." *Bulletin of the Atomic Scientists,* 26 (March 1970), pp. 2–8.

Lieberman, Leonard. "The Debate Over Race: A Study in the Sociology of Knowledge." *Phylon,* 29 (Summer 1968), pp. 127–141.

Litt, Edgar. "Civic Education, Community Norms, and Political Indoctrination." *American Sociological Review,* 28 (February 1963), pp. 69–75.

———. "Political Cynicism and Political Futility." *Journal of Politics,* 25 (May 1963), pp. 312–323.

Loehlin, John C.; Lindzey, Gardner; and Spuhler, J. N. *Race Differences in Intelligence.* San Francisco: Freeman, 1975.

Long, Samuel. "Cognitive-Perceptual Factors in the Political Alienation Process: A Test of Six Models." Paper presented at 34th Annual Meeting of Midwest Political Science Association, Chicago, April-May 1976.

———. "Political Disenchantment: A Cognitive-Perceptual Theory of Political Alienation." Paper presented at Annual Meeting of Southwestern Political Science Association, Dallas, April 1976.

McCarthy, John D., and Yancey, William L. "Uncle Tom and Mr. Charlie: Metaphysical Pathos in the Study of Racism and Personal Disorganization." *American Journal of Sociology,* 76 (January 1971), pp. 648–672.

McClosky, Herbert, and Schaar, John H. "Psychological Dimensions of Anomy." *American Sociological Review,* 30 (February 1965), pp. 14–40.

McPherson, J. Miller; Welch, Susan; and Clark, Cal. "The Stability and Reliability of Political Efficacy: Using Path Analysis to Test Alternative Models." *American Political Science Review,* forthcoming.

Matthews, Donald R., and Prothro, James W. *Negroes and the New Southern Politics.* New York: Harcourt, Brace, and World, 1966.

Merelman, Richard M. *Political Socialization and Educational Climates: A Study of Two School Districts.* New York: Holt, Rinehart, and Winston, 1971.

Miller, Arthur H. "Political Issues and Trust in Government: 1964–1970." *American Political Science Review,* 68 (September 1974), pp. 951–972.

———. "Rejoinder to 'Comment' by Jack Citrin: Political Discontent or Ritualism." *American Political Science Review,* 68 (September 1974), pp. 989–1001.

———; Brudney, Jeffrey; and Joftis, Peter. "Presidential Crises and Political Support: The Impact of Watergate on Attitudes Toward Institutions." Paper presented at 33rd Annual Meeting of Midwest Political Science Association, Chicago, May 1975.

Mirels, Herbert L. "Dimensions of Internal Versus External Control." *Journal of Consulting and Clinical Psychology,* 34 (April 1970), pp. 226–228.

Mokken, R. J. *A Theory and Procedure of Scale Analysis with Applications in Political Research.* The Hague: Mouton, 1971.

Morris, Milton D. *The Politics of Black Americans.* New York: Harper and Row, 1975.

Moynihan, Daniel P. *Maximum Feasible Misunderstanding: Community Action in the War on Poverty.* New York: Free Press, 1969.

Muller, Edward N. "A Test of a Partial Theory of Potential for Political Violence." *American Political Science Review,* 66 (September 1972), pp. 928–959.

———. "Cross-National Dimensions of Political Competence." *American Political Science Review,* 64 (September 1970), pp. 792–809.

———. "The Representation of Citizens by Political Authorities: Consequences for Regime Support." *American Political Science Review,* 64 (December 1970), pp. 1149–1166.

———, and Jukam, Thomas O. "On the Meaning of Political Support." *American Political Science Review,* forthcoming.

Niemi, Richard G. *How Family Members Perceive Each Other: Political and Social Attitudes in Two Generations.* New Haven, Conn.: Yale University Press, 1974.

———. "Political Socialization," in Jeanne N. Knutson (ed.), *Handbook of Political Psychology.* San Francisco: Jossey-Bass, 1973, pp. 117–138.

Nunnally, Jum C. *Psychometric Theory.* New York: McGraw-Hill, 1967.

Olsen, Marvin E. "Two Categories of Political Alienation." *Social Forces,* 47 (March 1969), pp. 288–299.

Orum, Anthony M.; Cohen, Roberta S.; Grasmuck, Sherri; and Orum, Amy W. "Sex, Socialization and Politics." *American Sociological Review,* 39 (April 1974), pp. 197–209.

Paige, Jeffrey M. "Political Orientation and Riot Participation." *American Sociological Review,* 36 (October 1971), pp. 810–820.

Pettigrew, Thomas F. *A Profile of the American Negro.* Princeton, N.J.: Van Nostrand, 1964.

Pinner, Frank A. "Parental Overprotection and Political Distrust." *Annals of the American Academy of Political and Social Science,* 361 (September 1965), pp. 58–70.

Polsby, Nelson W., and Wildavsky, Aaron B. *Presidential Elections: Strategies of American Electoral Politics.* 4th ed. New York: Scribner's, 1976.

Porter, Judith D. R. *Black Child, White Child: The Development of Racial Attitudes.* Cambridge, Mass.: Harvard University Press, 1971.

Powell, Gloria J., and Fuller, Marielle. "School Desegregation and Self-Concept." Paper presented at 47th Annual Meeting of American Orthopsychiatric Association, San Francisco, March 1970.

Prestage, Jewel L. "Black Politics and the Kerner Report: Concerns and Directions," in Norval D. Glenn and Charles M. Bonjean (eds.), *Blacks in the United States.* San Francisco: Chandler, 1969, pp. 538–549.

Proshansky, Harold, and Newton, Peggy. "The Nature and Meaning of Negro Self-Identity," in Martin Deutsch, Irwin Katz, and Arthur R. Jensen (eds.), *Social Class, Race, and Psychological Development.* New York: Holt, Rinehart, and Winston, 1968, pp. 178–218.

Remy, Richard C., and Nathan, James A. "The Future of Political Systems: What Young People Think." *Futures,* 6 (December 1974), pp. 463–476.

Renshon, Stanley Allen. *Psychological Needs and Political Behavior: A Theory of Personality and Political Efficacy.* New York: Free Press, 1974.

Riccards, Michael P. *The Making of the American Citizenry: An Introduction to Political Socialization.* New York: Chandler, 1973.

Robinson, John P.; Rusk, Jerrold G.; and Head, Kendra B. *Measures of Political Attitudes.* Ann Arbor, Mich.: Institute for Social Research, 1968.

Rosenberg, Morris. "The Logical Status of Suppressor Variables." *Public Opinion Quarterly,* 37 (Fall 1973), pp. 359–372.

———. *Society and the Adolescent Self-Image.* Princeton, N.J.: Princeton University Press, 1965.

———, and Simmons, Roberta G. *Black and White Self-Esteem: The Urban School Child.* Washington, D.C.: American Sociological Association, Arnold and Caroline Rose Monograph Series in Sociology, 1971.

Rotter, Julian B. "Generalized Expectancies for Internal versus External Control of Reinforcement." *Psychological Monographs: General and Applied,* 80 (Whole No. 609), 1966.

———. "Generalized Expectancies for Interpersonal Trust." *American Psychologist,* 26 (May 1971), pp. 443–452.

St. John, Nancy H. *School Desegregation: Outcomes for Children.* New York: Wiley-Interscience, 1975.

Schwartz, David C. *Political Alienation and Political Behavior.* Chicago: Aldine, 1973.

Schwartz, Sandra Kenyon. "Patterns of Cynicism: Differential Political Socialization among Adolescents," in David C. Schwartz and Sandra Kenyon Schwartz (eds.), *New Directions in Political Socialization.* New York: Free Press, 1975, pp. 188–202.

Sears, David O. *Political Attitudes Through the Life Cycle.* San Francisco: Freeman, forthcoming.

———. "Review of Langton, *Political Socialization:* Dawson and Prewitt, *Polit-*

ical Socialization; and Easton and Dennis, *Children in the Political System."* *Midwest Journal of Political Science,* 15 (February 1971), pp. 154–160.

————, and McConahay, John B. *The Politics of Violence: The New Urban Blacks and the Watts Riot.* Boston: Houghton Mifflin, 1973.

Seasholes, Bradbury. "Negro Political Participation in Two North Carolina Cities." Unpublished Ph.D. dissertation, University of North Carolina, 1962.

Seeman, Melvin. "On the Meaning of Alienation." *American Sociological Review,* 24 (December 1959), pp. 783–791.

Sheatsley, Paul B., and Feldman, Jacob J. "The Assassination of President Kennedy: A Preliminary Report on Public Reactions and Behavior." *Public Opinion Quarterly,* 28 (Summer 1964), pp. 189–215.

Siegel, Paul M. "On the Cost of Being a Negro." *Sociological Inquiry,* 35 (Winter, 1965), pp. 41–57.

Sigel, Roberta S. "An Exploration into Some Aspects of Political Socialization: School Children's Reactions to the Death of a President," in Martha Wolfenstein and Gilbert Kliman (eds.), *Children and the Death of a President: Multi-disciplinary Studies.* Garden City, N.Y.: Doubleday, Anchor Books, 1965, pp. 34–69.

————. "Bases of Political and Civic Involvement among Rural High School Youths—Internal/External Control and Involvement." Revised version of paper presented at 67th Annual Meeting of American Political Science Association, Chicago, September 1971.

————. "Psychological Antecedents and Political Involvement: The Utility of the Concept of Locus-of-Control." *Social Science Quarterly,* 56 (September 1975), pp. 315–323.

Smith, M. Brewster. *Social Psychology and Human Values.* Chicago: Aldine, 1969.

Sniderman, Paul M. *Personality and Democratic Politics.* Berkeley: University of California Press, 1975.

Spurlock, Jeanne. "Problems of Identification in Young Black Children—Static or Changing." *Journal of the National Medical Association,* 61 (November 1969), pp. 504–507, 532.

Stinchcombe, Arthur L. "Environment: The Cumulation of Effects Is Yet to Be Understood." *Harvard Educational Review,* 39 (Summer 1969), pp. 511–522.

Stokes, Donald E. "Popular Evaluations of Government: An Empirical Assessment," in Harlan Cleveland and Harold D. Lasswell (eds.), *Ethics and Bigness: Scientific, Academic, Religious, Political, and Military.* New York: Harper and Brothers, 1962, pp. 61–72.

Stone, William F. *The Psychology of Politics.* New York: Free Press, 1974.

Stryker, Sheldon S. "The Urban Scene: Observations from Research." *The Review* (Indiana University), 11 (Summer 1969), pp. 8–17.

Tapper, Ted. *Political Education and Stability: Elite Responses to Political Conflict.* New York: Wiley, 1976.

Thomas, Alexander, and Sillen, Samuel. *Racism and Psychiatry*. Secaucus, N.J.: Citadel Press, 1972.

Tumin, Melvin M. (ed.). *Race and Intelligence*. New York: Anti-Defamation League of B'nai B'rith, 1963.

U.S. Bureau of the Census. *1970 Census of Population: General Social and Economic Characteristics*. Washington, D.C.: U.S. Government Printing Office, 1972.

————. *Statistical Abstract of the United States, 1972*. 93d ed. Washington, D.C.: U.S. Government Printing Office, 1972.

U.S. Commission on Civil Rights. *Racial Isolation in the Public Schools: Volume 1*. Washington, D.C.: U.S. Government Printing Office, 1967.

Vaillancourt, Pauline Marie. "The Stability of Children's Political Orientations: A Panel Study." Paper presented at 66th Annual Meeting of American Political Science Association, Los Angeles, September 1970.

————. "Stability of Children's Survey Responses." *Public Opinion Quarterly*, 37 (Fall 1973), pp. 373–387.

Van den Berghe, Pierre L. *Race and Racism: A Comparative Perspective*. New York: Wiley, 1967.

Wattenberg, Ben J., and Scammon, Richard M. "Black Progress and Liberal Rhetoric." *Commentary*, 55 (April 1973), pp. 35–44.

Weissberg, Robert. "Political Efficacy and Political Illusion." *Journal of Politics*, 37 (May 1975), pp. 469–487.

————. *Political Learning, Political Choice, and Democratic Citizenship*. Englewood Cliffs, N.J.: Prentice-Hall, 1974.

————, and Joslyn, Richard. "Methodological Appropriateness in Political Socialization Research," in Stanley Allen Renshon (ed.), *Handbook of Political Socialization: Theory and Research*. New York: Free Press, forthcoming.

White, Elliott S. "The Author Responds." *Journal of Politics*, 32 (November 1970), pp. 992–993.

————. "Genetic Diversity and Political Life: Toward a Populational-Interaction Paradigm." *Journal of Politics*, 34 (November 1972), 1203–1242.

————. "Intelligence and Sense of Political Efficacy in Children." *Journal of Politics*, 30 (August 1968), pp. 710–731.

————. "Intelligence, Individual Differences and Learning: An Approach to Political Socialization." *British Journal of Sociology*, 20 (March 1969), pp. 50–68.

Wright, James D. *The Dissent of the Governed: Alienation and Democracy in America*. New York: Academic Press, 1976.

Yancey, William L.; Rigsby, Leo; and McCarthy, John D. "Social Position and Self-Evaluation: The Relative Importance of Race." *American Journal of Sociology*, 79 (September 1972), pp. 338–359.

Index